Napoleon Bonaparte: Master of War

The Great Man and his Great Battles

For almost two decades, Napoleon Bonaparte was the most feared, and revered, man in Europe. At the height of his power, the land under his control stretched from the Baltic to the Mediterranean, and encompassed most of Western Europe.

But how was it possible that a young Corsican, who spoke French with a strange accent, could become Emperor of the French at the age of just thirty-three and dominate Europe for a generation, defeating every army sent against him, until finally overwhelmed by the coalitions repeatedly mounted to oppose him?

In this far-reaching investigation, we examine Napoleon's art of war and that magnificent fighting force, the Imperial Guard, which grew from a small personal bodyguard to the size of a small army. We analyse his great battles, such as Marengo, Austerlitz, Jena and Wagram.

We also take a look at Napoleon's great Oriental adventure, which saw him conquer Egypt. He took with him artists and scientists, which led to the discovery of the Rosetta Stone and the deciphering of the Egyptian hieroglyphs.

Napoleon, however, took a step too far when he marched into Russia. The vast distances and the weather wrecked his army and he was never able to recover, and eventually his enemies proved too strong. France was invaded and he was compelled to abdicate.

Napoleon was not finished, though, and he returned from exile to lead France into war one more time, only for his army to be beaten beyond all hope of recovery in the muddy Flanders' fields at Waterloo. So, ended one of the most turbulent eras in history, one that, to this day, still bears his name. But his legacy lives on in the French legal and social systems and he remains as enigmatic a figure today as he was 200 years ago. Indeed, as this publication goes to press, Hollywood has announced that the Ridley Scott epic - *Napoleon* - starring Joaquin Phoenix is set for cinema release in November, 2023.

John Grehan
Editor

ORIGINALLY PUBLISHED 2018 CONTAINS MINOR UPDATES
ISBN: 978 1 80282 764 4
Editor: John Grehan
Senior editor, specials: Roger Mortimer
Email: roger.mortimer@keypublishing.com
Cover design: Steve Donovan
Design: Dan Jarman
Advertising Sales Manager: Brodie Baxter
Email: brodie.baxter@keypublishing.com
Tel: 01780 755131
Advertising Production: Becky Antoniades
Email: Rebecca.antoniades@keypublishing.com

SUBSCRIPTION/MAIL ORDER
Key Publishing Ltd, PO Box 300, Stamford, Lincs, PE9 1NA
Tel: 01780 480404
Subscriptions email: subs@keypublishing.com
Mail Order email: orders@keypublishing.com
Website: www.keypublishing.com/shop

PUBLISHING
Group CEO and Publisher: Adrian Cox
Published by
Key Publishing Ltd, PO Box 100, Stamford, Lincs, PE9 1XQ
Tel: 01780 755131
Website: www.keypublishing.com

PRINTING
Precision Colour Printing Ltd, Haldane, Halesfield 1, Telford, Shropshire. TF7 4QQ

DISTRIBUTION
Seymour Distribution Ltd, 2 Poultry Avenue, London, EC1A 9PU
Enquiries Line: 02074 294000.

We are unable to guarantee the bona fides of any of our advertisers. Readers are strongly recommended to take their own precautions before parting with any information or item of value, including, but not limited to money, manuscripts, photographs, or personal information in response to any advertisements within this publication.

© Key Publishing Ltd 2023
All rights reserved. No part of this magazine may be reproduced or transmitted in any form by any means, electronic or mechanical, including photocopying, recording or by any information storage and retrieval system, without prior permission in writing from the copyright owner. Multiple copying of the contents of the magazine without prior written approval is not permitted.

BELOW: *After another military victory, Napoleon takes the surrender of General Mack and the Austrians at Ulm on 20 October 1805.* (Anne S.K. Brown Military Collection, Brown University Library)

CONTENTS · NAPOLEON BONAPARTE

CONTENTS

6 FROM THE SUBLIME TO THE RIDICULOUS
A timeline exploring the life of Napoleon Bonaparte, from Corsican resistance fighter to conqueror of Europe.

12 'I BELIEVE MYSELF A SUPERIOR MAN'
The battle at the bridge at Lodi and the creation of the Napoleonic Legend.

20 ORIENTAL ADVENTURE
From the Nile to the Pyramids, the story of Napoleon's expedition to Egypt.

26 'NOT TONIGHT JOSÉPHINE'
The Women in Napoleon's life.

32 CHARLEMAGNE'S HEIR
Napoleon I, the Emperor of the French.

38 THE ARBITER OF VICTORY
The creation and gallantry of Napoleon's Imperial Guard, France's finest fighting force.

45 NAPOLEON'S GREATEST BATTLES
Introduced and selected by historian and author Robert Burnham, this gallery of paintings and prints details five battles that defined Napoleon: Marengo (14 June 1800); Austerlitz (2 December 1805); Jena-Auerstadt (14 October 1806); Friedland (14 June 1807); and Wagram (5–6 July 1809).

56 THE LEGION D'HONNÉUR
'It is with baubles that men are led' – the story of France's highest military and civil award.

Napoleon Bonaparte — Contents

ABOVE: *A portrait of Napoleon at the ascendency of his service to France, showing him as First Consul following the ceremony on 25 December 1799.* (Anne S.K. Brown Military Collection, Brown University Library)

58 NAPOLEON'S SPANISH ULCER
The War in the Iberian Peninsula.

64 NAPOLEON'S EMPIRE
It is usually said that Napoleon reached the height of his power in 1807, after his alliance with Tsar Alexander of Russia, but at that time his empire was still expanding, reaching its maximum extent in 1812 – just before its dramatic collapse.

66 BLOOD IN THE SNOW
The dramatic story of Napoleon's disastrous and costly invasion of Russia in 1812 and the long retreat that followed.

76 BATTLE OF THE NATIONS
The invasion of Russia had destroyed Napoleon's Grand Armée and presented his enemies with a chance to finally bring him down. The opposing sides met at the Saxon city of Leipzig, in what was to be the largest battle in Europe before the First World War.

83 ABDICATION AND EXILE
There was to be no heroic last stand in Paris; there would be no ruins under which the Bonapartes would die fighting. In the end, the fall of Napoleon's empire was quite peaceful and even civilised.

87 RETURN OF THE EAGLES – WATERLOO
The magical story of the young Corsican who rose to be an emperor and the most powerful man in Europe is one of the greatest of all time. Yet, there was to be a postscript, which culminated in one of the most memorable battles in history.

94 GONE BUT NOT FORGOTTEN
Napoleon's final exile and death, as well as his enduring legacy.

BELOW: *The battle for which Napoleon is perhaps most remembered – that at Waterloo on Sunday, 18 June 1815 – was also the one which finally sealed his fate. This depiction of one part of that epic battle shows British troops capturing the Eagle of the French 45th Line.* (Anne S.K. Brown Military Collection, Brown University Library)

From The Sublime To The Ridiculous

The Life of Napoleon Bonaparte
From Corsican Resistance fighter to Conqueror of Europe

MAIN PICTURE: *Napoleon on St Helena after his exile there on 22 June 1815.* (Anne S.K. Brown Military Collection, Brown University Library)

Napoleon Bonaparte — From The Sublime To The Ridiculous

Part of the large complex of the Ecole Militaire in Paris, where Napoleon enrolled on 17 October 1784. (Kiev Victor/Shutterstock)

FROM THE SUBLIME ...
Napoleon is reputed to have said, 'From the sublime to the ridiculous there is but one step', during the disastrous retreat from Moscow in 1812 - as detailed in Abbe de Pradt, *Histoire de l'Ambassade dans le Grand Duché de Varsovie en 1812* (Paris, 1815), pp.214-5.

15 August 1769
Napoleone di Buonaparte was born in Ajaccio, Corsica, the son of Carlo Maria Buonaparte, a minor Italian nobleman and lawyer. That same year France completed its conquest of Corsica.

17 May 1779
Having started his education at a boys' school in Ajaccio, followed by a brief spell at a religious school in Autun in France, Napoleon was accepted into the l'Ecole royale militaire de Brienne-le-Château, at the age of nine. An examiner there suggested that Napoleon would make a good sailor!

17 October 1784
Napoleon enrolled in the prestigious Ecole Militaire in Paris, graduating from there on 28 October 1785 with the rank of second lieutenant in the artillery Régiment de la Fère.

14 July 1789
The Paris mob stormed the Bastille and the French Revolution turned violent. Napoleon took leave of his regiment to return to Corsica, where he became involved in attempts to overturn the existing regime in favour of the Republicans. He was promoted to captain in his regiment, despite his absence.

29 August 1793
Having ingratiated himself with one of the leaders of the Revolution, Maximilien Robespierre, Napoleon was sent to take command of the French artillery around Toulon, which had been captured by the British. His successful handling of the artillery resulted in the British being driven away.

22 December 1793
Napoleon was promoted to the rank of Général de brigade, and placed in charge of the artillery of France's Armée d'Italie.

9 August 1794
When Robespierre fell from grace and was executed, Napoleon was imprisoned under suspicion of being one of Robespierre's supporters. He was released on 20 August.

21 April 1795
Napoleon became engaged to Désirée Clary, the daughter of a wealthy Marseille merchant.

5 October 1795
Napoleon saved the Directory from the Paris mob, with 'a whiff of grapeshot', and as a result was given his first command as a general, that of Armée de l'Ouest, but as this was involved in an internal struggle with Royalist supporters he declined the posting citing health reasons.

15 October 1795
After having met Joséphine de Beauharnais at the home of Paul Francois Barras, a member of the ruling Directory, Napoleon visited her for the first time at her home.

2 March 1796
Napoleon was given command of the entire French army in Italy.

9 March 1796
Napoleon married Joséphine, having broken off his engagement to Désirée Clary.

ABOVE: *The building in Ajaccio, Corsica, where Napoleon was born on 15 August 1769.* (Shutterstock)

ABOVE: *The plaque that can be seen on the walls of Napoleon's birthplace on Corsica.* (Shutterstock)

From The Sublime To The Ridiculous — Napoleon Bonaparte

General Bonaparte, surrounded by members of the Council of Five Hundred, during the coup d'état on 9 November 1799.

27 March 1796
Napoleon opened his first Italian campaign against Austria and Piedmont. Over the course of little more than a year, Napoleon won eighteen battles, took 150,000 prisoners, 540 cannon, and 170 standards. This drove Piedmont out of the war, forced Austria to sue for peace and brought about the end of the First Coalition against France. In December 1797, he returned to Paris as a national hero.

19 May 1798
Napoleon sailed from Toulon to embark on the conquest of Egypt. En route to Egypt he captured Malta.

21 July 1798
Napoleon won the Battle of the Pyramids against the ruling Mamelukes, and three days later Cairo was occupied by the French.

1 August 1798
At the Battle of Aboukir Bay, a British fleet under the command of Admiral Nelson destroyed the French ships which had taken Napoleon's army to Egypt.

August 23, 1799
During Napoleon's absence from Europe, a Second Coalition was formed against France, and French forces suffered a number of defeats. This, in turn, led to political unrest in Paris. Seeking to take advantage of this unsettled political situation, Napoleon abandoned his army in the East and returned to Paris.

9 November 1799
Napoleon took part in a bloodless coup d'etat which led to the overthrow of the Directory and the establishment of the Consulate as the new government of France, with himself as First Consul.

ABOVE: *The original treaty between the United States of America and the French Republic on 30 April 1803, which ceded the province of Louisiana to the United States.* (National Archives and Records Administration)

12 December 1799
Napoleon was elected as First Consul, the formal ceremony taking place on 25 December that year.

20 May 1800
Napoleon led his army across the Alps through the Great St Bernard Pass during the Second Italian Campaign.

14 June 1800
Napoleon secured a victory against Austrian forces at the Battle of Marengo. This was followed by a further French victory at Hohenlinden, which forced Austria to request an armistice. On 9 February 1801, Austria signed the Treaty of Lunéville and withdrew from the Second Coalition.

15 July 1801
The Concordat between France and Rome was signed, ending the schism between the French government and the Catholic Church.

25 March 1802
The Treaty of Amiens was signed with Britain, bringing peace to all of Europe for the first time in ten years.

4 August 1802
France adopted a new constitution, making Napoleon First Consul for life.

ABOVE: *Napoleon is formally sworn in as First Consul on 25 December 1799.*

ABOVE: *A commemorative stamp produced in 1903 to mark the centenary of the Louisiana Purchase on 30 April 1803, which shows the scale of the territory ceded to the United States.*

Napoleon Bonaparte  From The Sublime To The Ridiculous

The Battle of Elchingen, 14 October 1805. Elchingen's Monastry Church can clearly be seen in the background. (Anne S.K. Brown Military Collection, Brown University Library)

2 December 1804
Napoleon crowned himself Emperor in Notre-Dame Cathedral, Paris.

17 March 1805
The Kingdom of Italy was created, with Napoleon as its king.

14 October 1805
At the Battle of Elchingen, Napoleon's French forces, under Michel Ney, routed an Austrian corps led by Johann Sigismund Riesch.

16-19 October 1805
Napoleon surrounded a complete Austrian army at Ulm, forcing it to surrender with minimal losses.

21 October 1805
Napoleon received news that the combined French and Spanish fleets had been heavily defeated at the Battle of Trafalgar, ending any real possibility of an invasion of England.

2 December 1805
Napoleon achieved a stunning victory against Austria and Russia at the Battle of Austerlitz. On 26 December, Austria signed the Treaty of Pressburg, leading to the end of the Holy Roman Empire and the creation of the Confederation of the Rhine under French control. It also marked the effective end of the Third Coalition.

ABOVE: *Following the surrender of General Mack and the Austrians at Ulm on **20 October 1805**, Napoleon takes a moment to salute some of the enemy's wounded. This decisive French victory ensured the destruction of the Austrian Army in Bavaria, and French control of Bavaria followed.*

30 April 1803
At Napoleon's insistence, France sold Louisiana to the United States for a total of 68 million francs ($15 million), the treaty being signed in Paris on this date. After the signing of the Louisiana Purchase agreement, Robert Livingston, who signed on behalf of America, made this famous statement: 'We have lived long, but this is the noblest work of our whole lives ... From this day the United States take their place among the powers of the first rank.'

18 May 1803
Britain broke the terms of the Treaty of Amiens by declaring war on France. This marked the start of the Napoleonic Wars. Napoleon established a camp at Boulogne in preparation for the invasion of England.

18 May 1804
The Senate proclaimed Napoleon Emperor of the French.

19 May 1804
Napoleon established the Légion d'Honneur. The first investitures took place at Les Invalides on 14 July 1804.

ABOVE: *The Battle of Austerlitz underway on **2 December 1805** - Napoleon and his aides are about to receive a report from an officer galloping in from the left. (Anne S.K. Brown Military Collection, Brown University Library)*

ABOVE: *Napoleon, in the centre, on the battlefield of Austerlitz, **2 December 1805**. (Anne S.K. Brown Military Collection, Brown University Library)*

From The Sublime To The Ridiculous Napoleon Bonaparte

ABOVE: *The Battle of Eylau, 7-8 February 1807, was a bloody battle between Napoleon's Grande Armée and the Imperial Russian Army. This painting depicts French infantry, more specially the 14e Regiment, holding the line against Russian grenadiers who are attacking from right.* (Anne S.K. Brown Military Collection, Brown University Library)

7 October 1806
The Fourth Coalition was formed. Napoleon responded swiftly, defeating the Prussians at the twin battles of Jena and Auerstedt. Prussia was overrun and Berlin occupied by the French. Severe restrictions were imposed on Prussia's military strength. Napoleon introduced the Continental System, banning European countries from trading with Britain.

7-8 February 1807
Napoleon fought an inconclusive battle with the Russians at Eylau.

14 June 1807
Napoleon defeated the Russians at the Battle of Friedland.

7 July 1807
Czar Alexander I made peace with Napoleon through the signing of the Treaty of Tilsit. This led to the collapse of the Fourth Coalition.

22 July 1807
The Grand Duchy of Warsaw (Poland) was created. This was to be overseen by France.

19 November 1807
General Junot led a French army which invaded Portugal. The Portuguese royal family was rescued by the Royal Navy and taken to the Portuguese colony of Brazil. This marked the start of the Peninsular War.

20 February 1808
Marshal Murat marched into Spain.

2 May 1808
Rioting broke out in Madrid against the French. This was the beginning of Spain's War of Independence.

4 June 1808
Napoleon named his brother, Joseph Bonaparte, King of Spain, following the abdication of King Carlos IV.

21 August 1808
A British army under Sir Arthur Wellesley landed in Portugal and defeated Junot at the Battle of Vimeiro. Junot sought an armistice and under the terms of the subsequent Convention of Cintra, agreed to evacuate Portugal.

ABOVE: *The signing of the Treaties of Tilsit on 7 July 1807. Here Napoleon is depicted meeting with Alexander I of Russia on a raft in the middle of the River Nieman.*

16 January 1809
A British army under Sir John Moore entered Spain to help the Spaniards, but was chased out of the country by Napoleon. Moore was killed at Corunna, and the British were forced to evacuate Spain.

10 April 1809
A Fifth Coalition was formed, following which Austria struck first. Napoleon, though, won battles at Eckmühl and Ebelsberg. Napoleon was defeated at the Battle of Aspern-Essling.

5-6 July 1809
Napoleon achieved a decisive victory at Wagram, which led to the collapse of the Fifth Coalition.

15 December 1809
Napoleon divorced Joséphine.

2 April 1810
Bonaparte married Marie-Louise, Archduchess of Austria.

26 April 1810
After the British army under Wellesley (now Viscount Wellington) won a number of victories in Spain and Portugal, Napoleon despatched a large force under Marshal André Masséna to drive the British out of Portugal.

20 March 1811
Bonaparte and Marie-Louise enjoyed the birth of a son, Napoléon François Charles Joseph.

5 April 1811
Masséna's campaign in Portugal ended in failure and he retreated to Spain.

24 June 1812
Czar Alexander withdrew from the Continental System and Napoleon decided to invade Russia with his Grande Armée of more than 600,000 men.

ABOVE: *Napoleon's abdication on 4 April 1814.* (Anne S.K. Brown Military Collection, Brown University Library)

Napoleon Bonaparte — From The Sublime To The Ridiculous

22 July 1812
Wellington achieved a major victory at Salamanca and King Joseph Bonaparte was compelled to abandon Madrid.

7 September 1812
The Battle of Borodino resulted in approximately 44,000 Russian and 35,000 French dead, wounded or captured, and may have been the bloodiest day of battle in history up to that point in time. Although the French had won, the Russian army had accepted, and withstood, the major battle Napoleon had hoped would be decisive. Napoleon later wrote: 'The most terrible of all my battles was the one before Moscow. The French showed themselves to be worthy of victory, but the Russians showed themselves worthy of being invincible.'

14 September 1812
Having achieved costly victories at Smolensk and Borodino, Napoleon entered Moscow only to find the city abandoned and set on fire by the Russians. The Czar's forces withdrew into the heart of Russia and Napoleon was unable to bring about a decisive battle. As winter set in, he was compelled to abandon Moscow and retreat to France, suffering crippling losses during the retreat.

ABOVE: *Russian troops enter Paris on 31 March 1814 after Napoleon's forces had surrendered.*

ABOVE: *Following the formation of The Sixth Coalition on 28 February 1813, the months that followed saw Napoleon's forces on campaign. This painting depicts the French leader during the Campaign of 1813 receiving a drinking flask from grenadier. (Anne S.K. Brown Military Collection, Brown University Library.)*

28 February 1813
The Sixth Coalition was formed and Napoleon achieved remarkable victories at Lützen, Bautzen and Dresden.

16 October 1813
The Battle of Leipzig began. Also known as the Battle of the Nations, this was the largest battle fought on European soil before the First World War.

21 June 1813
Wellington defeated the French forces in Spain at the Battle of Vitoria. The French retreated to the Pyrenees.

January 1814
The Coalition forces, led by Russia, Prussia and Austria, entered France. Though Napoleon won a succession of brilliant victories, he was unable to halt the allied advance.

30 March 1814
The Battle of Paris began. After a day of fighting in the suburbs of the French capital, the defenders surrendered on 31 March.

2 April 1814
The Senate announced the end of the Empire.

4 April 1814
Napoleon abdicated. King Louis XVIII was restored to the French throne.

4 May 1814
Napoleon was exiled to the Mediterranean island of Elba. His wife and son sought refuge in Vienna.

1 March 1815
Napoleon escaped from Elba and landed at Golfe-Juan in the South of France.

20 March 1815
After a long march, Napoleon and his supporters entered the French capital on 20 March. King Louis fled to Belgium.

18 June 1815
Napoleon was declared 'disturber of the tranquillity of the world' and the major European powers vowed to fight until Napoleon was finally defeated. Prussian and Anglo-Netherlands armies formed on the borders of France which Napoleon attacked, only to be defeated at the Battle of Waterloo.

22 June 1815
Napoleon abdicated for the second time and was exiled to the South Atlantic island of St Helena.

15 July 1815
Napoleon surrendered to Captain Frederick Maitland of HMS *Bellerophon*, and was transported to Plymouth. Having arrived in Tor Bay, Napoleon was moved to the 74-gun third-rate ship of the line HMS *Northumberland* for the voyage to St Helena, it being felt that *Bellerophon*, due to her age, was unsuitable for the journey.

8 August 1815
Having embarked a suitable escort for its VIP cargo, HMS *Northumberland* sailed for the South Atlantic, reaching Jamestown, St Helena, on 16 October 1815.

ABOVE: *Sitting at a desk in a cabin of HMS Northumberland, Napoleon drafts his last will and testament while en route to St Helena, the warship having sailed from England on 8 August 1815.*

5 March 1821
Napoleon died at the age of just fifty-one.

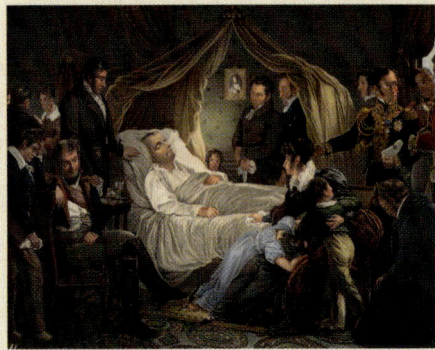
ABOVE: *Napoleon's last moments before his death on 5 March 1821. (Anne S.K. Brown Military Collection, Brown University Library.)*

'I Believe Myself A Superior Man'   Napoleon Bonaparte

'I Believe Myself A Superior Man'

The Bridge at Lodi and the Creation of the Napoleonic Legend

MAIN PICTURE: *Napoleon's artillery in action during the Siege of Toulon in 1793, the capture of which marked his first victory.* (Anne S.K. Brown Military Collection, Brown University Library)

RIGHT: *Edouard Detaille's depiction of Napoleon at Toulon in 1793.*

Napoleon Bonaparte — 'I Believe Myself A Superior Man'

Such is the mythology that has grown up around Napoleon, particularly in France where he is still revered, that in 1819 one author, Archbishop Whateley, mockingly wrote a book entitled *Historic Doubts Relative to Napoleon Buonaparte*[1], in which he suggested that no single person could have accomplished as much as Napoleon had in so short a space of time and he therefore cannot have really existed! 'The successive accounts of his exploits and conquests,' Whateley wrote, 'with dates, places and circumstances, which were spread throughout the nations, and at one time occupied the anxious attention of the civilised world were … the fictions of a lively fancy'. According to Whateley, Napoleon was a creation, a composite, an imaginary embodiment of the French national consciousness.

It is certainly true that, even in the twenty-first century, most visitors who take guided tours in Paris will be assailed by repeated references to Napoleon. Likewise, as anyone who has been to Waterloo will know, the main focus of the exhibits is on the man who lost the battle, not the victor.

Napoleon, of course, was real enough, though his early years, growing up in French-occupied Corsica as the son of a minor Italian noble, were hardly distinguished. When he went to school in France he was ridiculed for his Corsican accent and, unsurprisingly, was often involved in fights, becoming something of a loner. He began to gain confidence, and demonstrate something of the brilliant mind that would reveal itself fully in the years to come, at the École Royale Militaire in Paris. Upon graduation, he applied for a position in the artillery, the most technical of the three main arms of the Army. Only four from his school were granted places in the artillery, and Napoleon was one of them. It would be Napoleon's use of artillery which would become a major feature of his innovative battlefield tactics in the years ahead.

He took up his first posting with the Régiment de la Fère at Valence on 3 November 1785, but there were turbulent times ahead for both Napoleon and France. His father, Carlo, had died on 28 February that same year, leaving his family penniless; and France would be torn apart by violent and bloody Revolution, with the great monarchies of Europe declaring war on the Revolutionaries. It would be the Revolution, however, which would present Napoleon with opportunities not possible in more tranquil times. ➤

ABOVE: *Also entitled* Le souper de Beaucaire, *this painting depicts the meeting with the merchants that led to Napoleon writing the pamphlet of the same name – and which brought him to the attention of Maximilien Robespierre.*

'I Believe Myself A Superior Man' — Napoleon Bonaparte

ABOVE: *The destruction of the French fleet at Toulon, 18 December 1793.* (Anne S.K. Brown Military Collection, Brown University Library)

The First Victory – Taking Toulon

After a brief and ultimately unsatisfactory foray into Corsican politics, which led to his family having to flee the island leaving behind all its property, Napoleon returned to France. By this time a committed revolutionary, he wrote a political pamphlet, *Le souper de Beaucaire*, in support of the Revolution. Based on discussions he had with four merchants, this booklet brought him to the attention of the notorious leader of the ruling National Convention, Maximilien Robespierre. As a result, Napoleon was given his first command – with the artillery of the forces besieging the hugely important port of Toulon.

Royalist sympathisers had taken control of

RIGHT: *Napoleon directing the fighting during the Siege of Toulon.* (Anne S.K. Brown Military Collection, Brown University Library)

BELOW: *An engraving that shows the British evacuation of Toulon in December 1793.* (Anne S.K. Brown Military Collection, Brown University Library)

Toulon and appealed to the Anglo-Spanish fleet, led by Admiral Samuel Hood, for help. On 28 August 1793, the British and Spanish ships sailed into Toulon and took control of what was France's main naval port and arsenal where twenty-six ships-of-the-line, or around one third of France's naval strength, were berthed.

This was a serious blow to the National Convention at a time when Britain, Austria, Spain, Prussia, Portugal and a host of Italian countries were ranged against France in the First Coalition. Revolutionary armies were consequently despatched immediately to take back Toulon. But with the guns of more than sixty Allied warships and some 22,000 soldiers defending its fortifications, there was little the troops under General Jean Carteaux could do, other than lay siege to the port. That was until Napoleon arrived.

Napoleon Bonaparte — 'I Believe Myself A Superior Man'

TOP: *General Bonaparte gives his orders at the Battle of Lodi, 10 May 1796. The bridge over the River Adda dominates the scene.*

BOTTOM: *A contemporary satirical cartoon entitled 'Napoleon Working the Gun at Toulon'. (Anne S.K. Brown Military Collection, Brown University Library)*

Napoleon quickly assessed the situation. He saw that simply delivering frontal assaults upon the port's defences would achieve nothing. What he also saw was that Fort Éguillette, on the bay's western promontory, dominated both Toulon's inner and outer harbours. Napoleon had found the key that would unlock Toulon. 'Take L'Éguillette,' he told Carteaux, 'and within a week you are in Toulon'.[2] Rather than drive the Allied warships out, he would trap them in.

Carteaux, somewhat reluctantly, followed Napoleon's advice, but attacked with a weak force which was repelled by the Allies. All that Carteaux managed to do was make Hood realise the danger his forces would find themselves in if the fort fell into French hands. The Allies quickly erected a strong collection of earthworks to defend the promontory. But Napoleon was not to be deterred. He arranged for artillery to be brought from as far afield as Monaco, and established a battery powerful enough to dominate the guns in the newly-erected defences.

By 17 December, Napoleon had subdued the Allied artillery and was ready to order the attack. In a vicious night-time struggle, the British-held redoubts were taken, with Napoleon leading the final assault, being wounded, though not seriously, in the thigh by a British infantry sergeant's pike.

The next day, the Allied commanders, seeing that their ships would be trapped if they remained in Toulon, promptly prepared to escape. The Allies wrecked much of the French fleet in the harbour and attempted to destroy the arsenal, before departing on the 19th. Napoleon had won his first battle, just as he had predicted.

Napoleon was promoted to the rank of général de brigade and, in April 1795, he was assigned to the Armée de l'Ouest, which was engaged in supressing dissident Royalists in the Vendée region of France. Not only was this not the kind of operation which Napoleon wished to be involved in, it also meant taking command of an infantry brigade, which he saw as demotion from that of artillery general. He declined the posting. Instead he was employed in the Bureau of Topography, which was, in essence, the department of war planning. There, he focused much of his attention on the failing campaign in Italy. But it was not an office job Napoleon sought. Fate, though, was about to point her fickle finger in his direction.

A Whiff of Grapeshot

Political turmoil continued to rage throughout France, and in October 1795, following a controversial change in the administration of the government, the Royalists moved against the National Convention. With the commander of the Paris garrison, General Jacques-François de Menou, also indicating that he sympathised with the rebels, it looked as if the government would fall. But also in

'I Believe Myself A Superior Man'   Napoleon Bonaparte

Bonaparte, in the centre, in discussion with other senior officers during the fighting to capture the bridge at Lodi. (Anne S.K. Brown Military Collection, Brown University Library)

Paris was a certain artillery general.

One of the leaders of the ruling body, Paul Barras, turned to Napoleon for help. Napoleon agreed, but only on the condition that he was given complete freedom of action. When this was accepted, Napoleon ordered a young sous-lieutenant, Joachim Murat, to bring the cannon of the National Guard from the Camp des Sablons, on the outskirts of Paris, to the centre of the city, before the rebels had the same idea.

Murat returned with forty guns, which Napoleon set up to cover the approaches to the Tuileries. 'The danger was imminent,' Napoleon later wrote, '40,000 well-armed and well-organised National Guards were in the field and enraged against the Convention. The regular troops entrusted with the Convention's defence were few in number, and might easily be led away by the feelings of the people surrounding them.'[3] There was a prolonged stand-off, but then, at 16.45 hours on 5 October, the rebels charged – straight into the muzzles of Napoleon's guns. The attackers were mowed down in scores. With what Napoleon euphemistically called 'a whiff of grapeshot', he ruthlessly crushed the revolt. Around 1,400 Frenchmen lay dead in the streets of Paris.

For a second time Napoleon had saved the Revolution, and his name was on every Frenchman's lips. He was made Commander-in-Chief of the armée de l'Intérieur, and then, on 2 March 1796, he was given his first real combat command – in charge of the French army of Italy. He would have the chance to put the plans he had drawn up in the Topography Department into practise.

A Bridge to Cross

Though this new posting may sound like a wonderful position for the young Napoleon to be given – defending France's southern flank against the combined might of Austria and Sardinia-Piedmont – in reality, the armée d'Italie was in a deplorable state; many of its battalions were without shoes and carrying

ABOVE: *A depiction of another of Napoleon's victories that led to the Treaty of Campo Formio – the Battle of Arcole. Fought between French and Austrian forces on 15-17 November 1796, the battle saw Napoleon's men capture a bridge over the River Adige.* (Anne S.K. Brown Military Collection, Brown University Library)

BELOW: *A panoramic painting of the Siege of Toulon, the city visible in the distance.*

NAPOLEON BONAPARTE 'I BELIEVE MYSELF A SUPERIOR MAN'

muskets without bayonets. The men were half-starved and mutinous, and had been reduced to little more than 37,000 effectives out of an original 106,000. They were out-numbered by the comparatively well-provided enemy. Little wonder then, that when Napoleon took up his new command in Nice on 27 March 1796, he appealed more to the soldiers' needs than that of their country. 'I will lead you into the most fertile plains on earth. Rich provinces, opulent towns, all shall be at your disposal,' he claimed.[4] Now he had to prove it.

The campaign would, initially, be focussed along the passes of the Alps, with the Austrians and Sardinians, approximately 52,000 strong under General Beaulieu, placed to block these routes into Italy. It was this dispersal of the enemy forces which would play into Napoleon's hands. Using his central position, Napoleon, in the words of one historian, 'attacked, counterattacked, and pursued and harassed his stronger adversaries without respite, until he broke their resolve and induced them to abandon their missions'.[5]

His first move was to isolate the Sardinians from their Austrian allies. Napoleon often fought against stronger enemies, but his aim was always to achieve numerical superiority on the battlefield. This would be achieved through surprise and speed. In April 1796, the Austrians would be the first to experience this.

Though the Austrians moved first, Napoleon counter-attacked, defeating the Austrians at Montenotte and then Millesimo, driving a wedge between the Coalition armies, which enabled him to fall upon Feldmarschall-Leutnant Coli's Sardinians at Mondovi. A week later, the defeated Sardinians asked for an armistice and withdrew from the war.

Napoleon could now concentrate all his strength on the Austrians, and, on 10 May, the French caught up with their opponents at the River Po. General Beaulieu hoped to be able to hold the line of the river until he could be supported from Austria. Napoleon was determined not to give Beaulieu that chance. Though he could not stop Beaulieu from withdrawing behind the Po, Napoleon wanted to get across the river, and bring the Austrians to battle, before they became too well-established.

By the artist Antoine-Jean Gros, this painting depicts Napoleon, Tricolour in hand, on the bridge at Arcole during the fighting in November 1796.

There were three places where Napoleon could cross the Po, and he planned to send a diversionary force to attempt to cross the river at one point, before then launching his main attack further downstream. The operation went well, and the French were quickly across the Po. But Beaulieu was not going to stand and fight and he withdrew as fast as he could, hoping to reach the bridge over the River Adda at Lodi ahead of the French.

Napoleon gave chase, hounding his men on, but when they came within sight of the Adda most of the Austrians were safely across the river, leaving just a rear guard of 10,000 men on the southern bank to cover the crossing under General Sebottendorf. Napoleon desperately needed to bring Beaulieu to battle before he was reinforced.

Sebottendorf had positioned three of his battalions, supported by twelve cannon, to defend the bridge and the causeway leading up to it. Six of these guns were placed at the eastern end of the bridge, with the others on either side of the causeway. Any attempt to take the bridge would be met with a hail of canister as they approached the river and, if any attackers had survived that onslaught to reach the bridge, they would then have to advance directly upon the guns at the end of the bridge. It would be certain slaughter. But it would not stop Bonaparte.

Firstly, he sent detachments up and down the Adda to see if there was a ford by which his troops could cross to outflank the Austrian position. This, though, was a long-shot, and if Napoleon did not act quickly, Beaulieu would once again escape his clutches. So, he formed his grenadiers into a column, and, in true classical fashion, delivered an encouraging speech, then launched them at the bridge. ➤

ABOVE: *Tranquil today, this is the current bridge over the River Adda at Lodi and the scene of bitter fighting on 10 May 1796.*

17

'I Believe Myself A Superior Man' NAPOLEON BONAPARTE

With the cry of '*Vive la République*' and, for the first time '*Vive Bonaparte!*', the grenadiers charged along the causeway through a hail of lead, and onto the bridge. There, however, they could go no further, being beaten back by the storm of Austrian shot from the cannon at the eastern end.

Yet, rather than be dismayed at being repulsed, the grenadiers, led by officers who would become famous marshals of France, such as Masséna and Berthier, seemed inspired and, almost immediately, they launched a second attack. This time, the French artillery opened fire on the enfilading Austrian guns, enabling the attacking column to reach the bridge in formation. The French column then stormed across the bridge. In the face of such terrifying determination, the Austrians gave way, and Napoleon's troops reached the eastern side. They had seized the bridge at Lodi. It had cost them 350 men.

It was a remarkable achievement, and it was at Lodi that Napoleon realised that he could achieve something monumental. Just a few days after the battle he confided to August de Marmont, another who would one day carry a marshal's baton, 'In our days no one has conceived anything great; it is for me to set the example'.

Lodi was not the decisive battle that Napoleon sought, as Beaulieu's army was able to escape largely intact. But it had instilled a belief in his men that they were superior to their enemies and that under Napoleon's leadership nothing could stand in their away; and so it proved. For, after Lodi, success followed success, with the French government realising that something special was happening beyond the Alps and sending Napoleon strong reinforcements.

Beaulieu tried yet again to hold the line of a river, this time the Mincio. Once more, the Austrian line was broken, at the Battle Borgetto. Beaulieu was forced to retreat, leaving the key fortress of Mantua to be surrounded by the French. Over the course of the next eight months, the Austrians undertook four separate relief attempts of Mantua, each of which met defeat at the hands of Napoleon's forces in battles at Lonato, Castiglione, Rovereto, Bassano and Arcole.

Vive Napoleon!

During this time Napoleon attacked and defeated the army of Pope Pius VI. The French Revolutionary leaders had declared that all Church land belonged to the state, and on 23 November 1793, churches were closed, being converted into warehouses or even stables. Following these principles, Napoleon insisted that Pius should renounce his temporal power, and when the Pope refused to be cowed, Napoleon arrested him.

On 2 February 1797, Napoleon finally captured Mantua, after the defeat of the last relief attempt at the Battle of Rivoli, with the Austrians surrendering 18,000 men. Napoleon then invaded the Tyrol, and at the same time other French armies, under generals Moreau and Hoche, invaded Germany. It was all too much for Austria, and in April Emperor Francis II sued for peace, bringing about the collapse of the First Coalition against France.

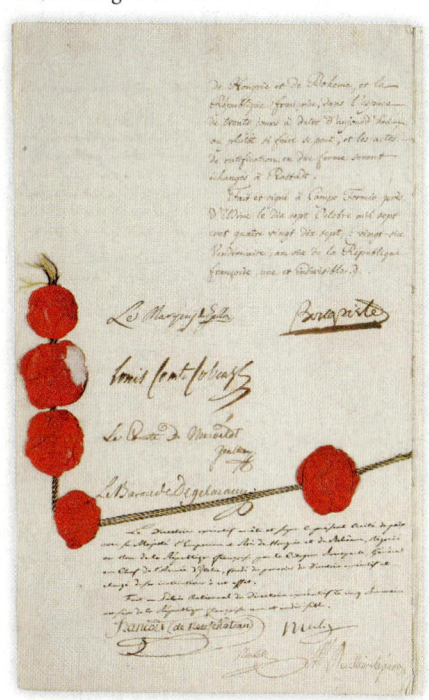

ABOVE: *The actual Treaty of Campo Formio signed by Napoleon.* (French National Archives)

BELOW: *A relief panel on the Arc de Triomphe in Paris which commemorates the Battle of Arcole.*

ABOVE: *Napoleon, again clutching a Tricolour, leads his men in the attack on the bridge over the River Adige at Arcole.*

In October 1797, Austria signed the Treaty of Campo Formio, with General Bonaparte signing on behalf of France. Austria had to hand over some of its territories to France, including Belgium (the Austrian Netherlands) and islands in the Adriatic, and its Italian possessions became independent republics under French control.

Napoleon's achievements were astonishing, and he returned to Paris to wild acclaim, his fame, and his future assured, and his ambitions unrestrained. He had seen that men believed in him and would follow him anywhere.

Though he wore his men out with marching, and made ceaseless demands on their courage and endurance, from Lodi onwards Napoleon was idolised by them, creating those vital personal bonds which would cause his troops to march to certain death, crying, '*Vive Bonaparte!*'.[6] The Italian campaign, and that crucial crossing of the River Adda, had made Napoleon realise he was destined for greatness, telling Emmanuel Las Cases,[7] 'it was only on the evening after Lodi that I started to believe myself a superior man'.[8] At Lodi the legend had been born, and soon the cries of his men would not be for General Bonaparte, they would be for the Emperor Napoleon. ❖

NOTES:
1. It was published in 1844 by the American Sunday-School Union, in Philadelphia.
2. Quoted in Frank McLynn, *Napoleon, A Biography* (Pimlico, London, 1997), p.73.
3. Somerset de Chair (Ed.), *Napoleon on Napoleon, An Autobiography of the Emperor* (Cassell, London, 1992), p.89.
4. Quoted in Emil Ludwig, *Napoleon* (George Allen, London, 1935), p.56.
5. David Chandler, *The Campaigns of Napoleon* (Macmillan, New York, 1966), p.128.
6. ibid, p.130.
7. Las Cases accompanied Napoleon to St Helena, where he recorded the former emperor's accounts of his campaigns.
8. Steven Englund, *Napoleon, A Political Life* (Scribner, New York, 2004), p.108.

VISIT OUR ONLINE SHOP

shop.keypublishing.com/battlesthatchangedtheworld

Key Shop

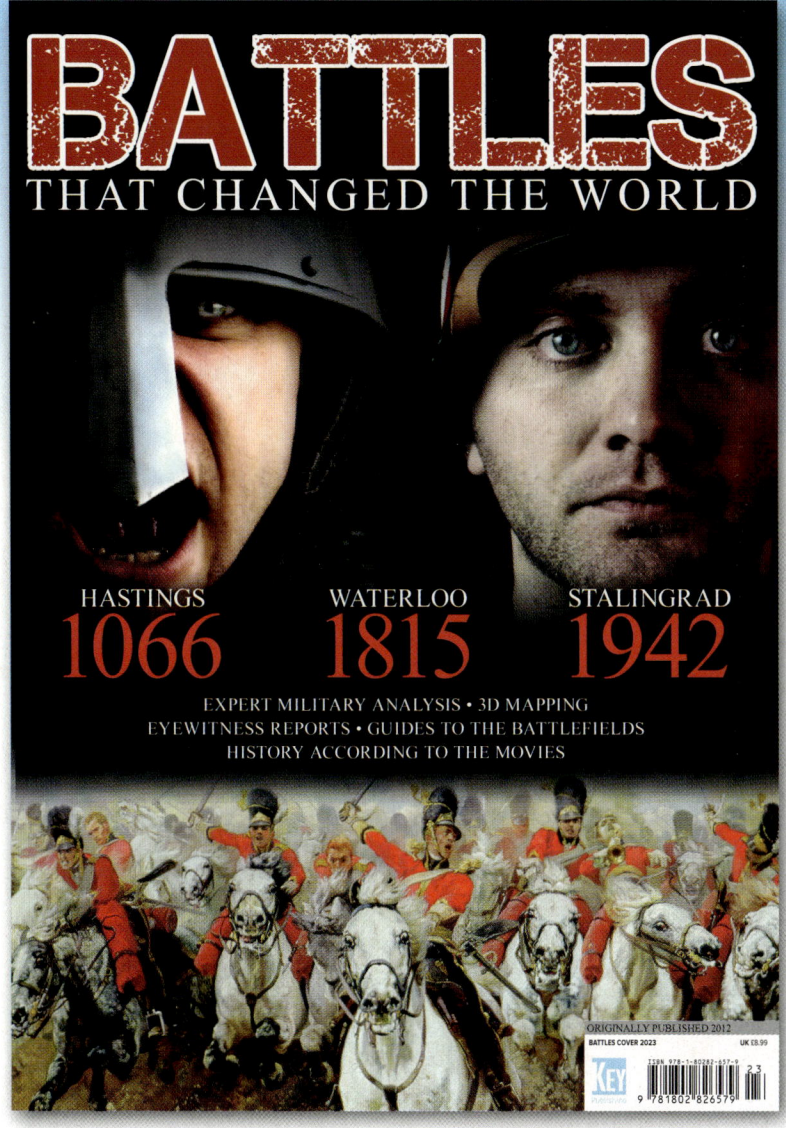

This 100-page special publication sees Robert Kershaw, one of the UK's leading battle historians, take a unique look at three major battles from world history. Covering the Battle of Hastings (1066), the Battle of Waterloo (1815) and the Battle of Stalingrad (1941/2) it features conflict introductions and narratives complete with detailed maps and battle diagrams.

The title includes portraits of the combatants including how they lived in the field, their daily activities and battle experiences. And the author offers a war correspondent's view of the battles, with detailed maps to immerse you in the battlefield experience. Originally released in 2012, Battles That Changed The World is a must-read for anyone with an interest in military history.

Scan me to order!

ONLY £8.99 + FREE P&P

SUBSCRIBERS don't forget to use your **£2 OFF DISCOUNT CODE!**

IF YOU ARE INTERESTED IN **WORLD HISTORY** YOU MAY ALSO WANT TO ORDER...

 £8.99

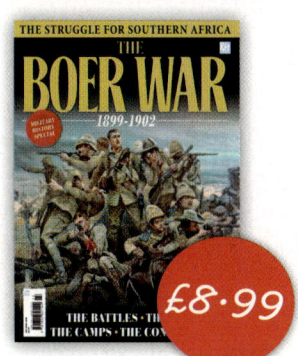 £8.99

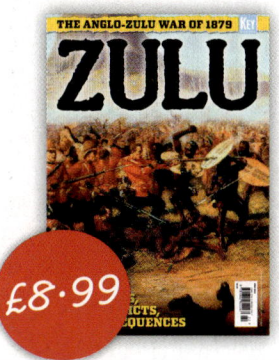 £8.99

 £8.99

FREE P&P* when you order online at...

shop.keypublishing.com/battlesthatchangedtheworld

Call +44 (0)1780 480404 *(Monday to Friday 9am-5.30pm GMT)*

Also available from **W.H Smith** and all leading newsagents.

*Free 2nd class P&P on all UK & BFPO orders. Overseas charges apply.

ORIENTAL ADVENTURE

Napoleon's Expedition to Egypt

The collapse of the Coalition after the signing of the Treaty of Campo Formio left only Great Britain (and her oldest ally, Portugal) at war with France. It was believed, correctly as it transpired, that at the first opportunity Britain would use its great wealth to encourage the nations of Europe to join again in a bid to bring down the Revolutionary government. Somehow, Britain had to be defeated.

Though an 'Army of England' was formed, command of which was given to Napoleon, there was little chance of getting to grips with Britain, defended as it was by the 'wooden walls' of the Royal Navy. Britain, however, owed much of its prosperity to its international trade, particularly with its companies in India, and if Britain was vulnerable it was beyond her own shores. France, of course, could not hope to transport a large army to somewhere like India by sea, but General Bonaparte conceived another plan which would both enhance France's trading opportunities in the Orient and impede Britain's access to the East. His plan was to capture Egypt, from where French armies could march on India and link hands with France's few friends in the sub-continent, and French merchants could establish trade routes to the East.[1] 'The day is not far distant,' he told the Directory in the summer of 1797, 'when we should appreciate the necessity, in order really to destroy England, of seizing Egypt.' The Directory's Foreign Minister, Talleyrand, agreed with Bonaparte: 'By establishing France in Africa we shall guarantee the peace of Europe.'[2]

This was obviously a long-shot, but others in France had long considered an expedition to Egypt and his proposal was readily seized upon. As far as the Directory was concerned, the idea of sending off the popular and clearly ambitious young general to such distant lands (from which he might not return) was not without its merits.

The expedition would not merely be a military operation. Egypt would be liberated from the despotic rule of the Mamelukes, and the ideals of the Revolution – liberty, equality and fraternity – would be spread to the Orient. Along with soldiers would go 500 mechanics, engineers, architects, authors, mathematicians and interpreters. This was the age of enlightenment and France would enlighten the Orient.

Battle of the Nile

From Marseilles, Toulon, Genoa, Ajaccio and Civita Vecchia the armada – thirteen ships of the line, fourteen frigates, and 400 transports – sailed east carrying in the region of 30,000 soldiers drawn from forces serving in Italy, Rome, Corsica, Switzerland and northern France. With them went sixty field guns and forty heavy siege guns.

The first objective of the expedition which, after some delay, set off on 19 May 1798, was the island of Malta, where the ships needed to take on water and supplies. The French were told by the governing Knights of St John that only two foreign ships at a time were permitted to enter Valetta's Grand Harbour.

This was clearly impractical for a fleet of almost 450 ships, so Napoleon ordered his troops to land and seize the island. This was accomplished with little effort, and on 11 June Malta became part of the French Republic. After the fleet's stocks were replenished, Napoleon sailed on 19 June, destination Alexandria. But news of the French expedition had reached London, and a British fleet under the command of Rear Admiral Horatio Nelson was scouring the Mediterranean in search of the French ships.

Nelson's warships, sailing twice as fast as Napoleon's lumbering transports, actually reached Alexandria first, but finding no trace of the French fleet, the British set off again – the last brig departing just two hours before the leading French ship arrived within sight of the Egyptian port. Napoleon lost no time in disembarking his troops. By 3 July the entire force was safely ashore, and Admiral Brueys took his squadron from the restricted port to the larger anchorage of Aboukir Bay. It was there that, almost a month later, Nelson found the French ships.

As night closed in on 1 August, so did the British fleet. By dawn the next day, Brueys was dead and his squadron sunk, disabled or dispersed. What became known as the Battle of the Nile was one of Nelson's most decisive victories and it meant that Napoleon's army was stranded in the Orient. ➤

MAIN PICTURE: *By the artist Antoine-Jean Gros, this image shows Napoleon during the Battle of the Pyramids with a number of Ottoman casualties to his front. Murad's losses were far heavier than Napoleon's – perhaps as many as 3,000 of the irreplaceable Mamluk cavalry and unknown numbers of infantry.* (Anne S.K. Brown Military Collection, Brown University Library)

Oriental Adventure   Napoleon Bonaparte

Battle of the Pyramids

Napoleon, on the other hand, had won a battle of his own. After the landing at Alexandria, he had marched upon Cairo. The forces that opposed the invaders were led by Murad and Ibrahim Bey who, between them, commanded an elite force of 6,000 mounted Mameluks with 15,000 mounted *fellahin* militia and possibly as many as 100,000 other warriors. But the Mameluks had made the fatal error of dividing their forces, with Murad on the left bank of the Nile and Ibrahim on the right.

The opposing forces met nine miles from the Pyramids of Giza. As the battle was about to begin, Napoleon famously encouraged his men with the words, 'Forward! Remember that from those monuments yonder forty centuries look down upon you'.

The Battle of the Pyramid's opened with a furious charge by the Mameluke cavalry. Napoleon's force, which had been reduced by sickness and the need to garrison Alexandria to possibly little more than 20,000, should have been swept away in the open desert by the Mamelukes, but Napoleon had a trick up his sleeve.

The accepted means by which infantry might resist a cavalry charge was by forming battalion squares. But in such wide expanses against such a numerous foe, these little squares might easily be overwhelmed. So, Napoleon arranged his army with one flank resting securely on the River Nile, and then arranging his men into five huge hollow divisional squares, though actually they were more rectangular in shape. The army's baggage wagons were put inside the squares, with cannon placed at each corner. The army's other flank lay on a large village,

MAIN PICTURE: *A dramatic depiction of the Battle of the Pyramids, which can be seen in the background, as it unfolded on 21 July 1798. Engulfed by the west bank portion of the city of Cairo, nothing remains of the battlefield today.* (Musée National des Châteaux de Versailles)

Napoleon Bonaparte | Oriental Adventure

FAR LEFT: *Troops for Napoleon's Egyptian offensive embarking in their transports at Toulon, from where they eventually sailed on 19 May 1798.* (Anne S.K. Brown Military Collection, Brown University Library)

MIDDLE FAR LEFT: *Thomas Whitcombe's painting of the moment that the French flagship, l'Orient, exploded during the Battle of the Nile. Though the explosion is also often presented as a turning point of the battle, some state that the battle had already been won by this point. Shortly after the battle, Nelson was presented with a coffin carved from a piece of l'Orient's main mast, which had been taken back to Britain for this purpose; he was put inside this coffin after his death at the Battle of Trafalgar.* (Historic Military Press)

LEFT: *The British fleet bears down on the anchored French during the opening stages of the Battle of the Nile on 1 August 1798.* (Historic Military Press)

BELOW: *Napoleon urging his troops on during the Battle of the Pyramids, which ended as a decisive victory in his favour.* (Anne S.K. Brown Military Collection, Brown University Library)

which Napoleon garrisoned with a detachment of cavalry and grenadiers.

At 15.30 hours on 21 July, Murad Bey's Mamelukes charged with a ferocious yell against the French right. The squares held their shape, and the men their nerve, as the Egyptian horsemen split into three columns and swarmed around and between the French formations.

Peppered by the muskets of the French infantry and a howitzer fired from the central of the five squares into the mass of horsemen, the Mamelukes were driven towards the village on the French right. This gave Napoleon his opportunity to move forward with his left along the Nile, supported by French gunboats moving upstream, to fall on the now isolated wing of Murat's force in the village of Embabeh.

The Arabs and the Mamelukes saw that they were trapped in the village which quickly became a killing ground. In desperation, some of the Mamelukes jumped into the river to try and escape to join Ibrahim on the other side, with many hundreds being drowned and thousands of others shot or bayonetted. The French had less than 300 casualties.

A Just Ruler

There seems to be no doubting that for all his powerful personal ambitions, Napoleon believed in the principles of *Liberté, Equalité, Fraternité*, in so far as it suited his aims. He, therefore, attempted to portray his invasion of Egypt in those terms, as the man who would bring liberty to the Egyptians who had suffered under centuries of Ottoman and Mameluke domination. But such libertarian ideals were lost on the Imams, the spiritual leaders of the country, who regarded the infidels, with their excessive consumption of liquor, to be barbarians. ➢

ORIENTAL ADVENTURE NAPOLEON BONAPARTE

The one thing that did impress the Egyptian leaders was the Institut d'Egypte, composed of the academics who had accompanied the expedition. It was formed on 22 August, with its members travelling with the French troops to every corner of the country, studying the remarkable monuments of Ancient Egypt and founding the science of Egyptology.

Amongst the projects undertaken by the *savants* was one that Napoleon was particularly interested in – the rediscovery of the Canal of the Pharaohs. This was built, or at least started by, King Necho II in the 6th century BC, though it is not known when it was completed or first used. This ancient structure linked the Nile to the Red Sea. The prospect of re-building the canal and opening a route from the Mediterranean through the Red Sea into the Indian Ocean was an exciting one. Not only would it mean that French ships could sail to the Far East again, but also that travelling times between India and Europe would be considerably reduced, thus offering real commercial advantages to French merchants. It would be in this manner that the English would be beaten.

In November 1798 Napoleon sent General Bon to occupy the town of Suez on the Red Sea. Bon fortified the town against Arab insurgents, and on Christmas Eve Napoleon joined him, along with a large retinue, which included the members of the Institut d'Egypte as well as some prominent figures from Cairo. Six days later Napoleon's party set out to look for the remains of the ancient canal. According to the official version of events, it was General Bonaparte who first found what was left of Necho's waterway. His troops even marched for four leagues along the canal itself.

Though survey work was undertaken, and estimates to build another canal were calculated, it was another fifty years before Napoleon's dream was realised, and it was French engineers that built the Suez Canal we know today.

It was another discovery, much smaller in size than Necho's canal, but with possibly even greater historical impact, with which Napoleon's expedition to Egypt is most widely known. This discovery occurred on 15 July 1799, when soldiers under the command of a Colonel d'Hautpoul were working on the fortifications of Fort Julien which was situated just a couple of miles to the north-east of the port-city of Rosetta (today called Rashid). The soldiers uncovered a large stone slab covered

ABOVE: *The Institut d'Égypte first met on 24 August 1798, with Bonaparte himself as vice-president. The building itself was burnt down on 17 December 2011, as a consequence of street clashes that erupted during the Egyptian revolution that broke out earlier that year. Despite the valiant efforts of fire fighters and protestors from all sides, a number of important works were lost when fire swept through the Institute. This picture shows the rebuilding work underway.* (Courtesy of Mohamed Ouda)

TOP RIGHT: *The Rosetta Stone can today be viewed by visitors to the British Museum, it having eventually fallen into the hands of British troops.*

BELOW: *Napoleon before the Sphinx during his campaign in Egypt.* (Art Renewal Center)

NAPOLEON BONAPARTE | ORIENTAL ADVENTURE

with inscriptions. Lieutenant Pierre-François Bouchard immediately saw that it was an object of some importance and he drew d'Hautpoul's attention to the find.

The clearly damaged and irregular slab was 3 feet 8 inches high at its highest point, 2 feet 5.8 inches wide, and 11 inches thick. The two officers alerted General Menou at Rosetta to their find, and the general passed the news on to the scholars of the Institut d'Égypte.

The stone was recovered from the construction site and transported to Cairo for examination. It did not take the members of the Institute long to see that the stone carried three different forms of writing, one being Egyptian hieroglyphs, which had proven to be indecipherable, and another being ancient Greek. The third set of inscriptions remained unidentified at this early stage. It was very soon apparent that all three were inscriptions of the same text. Though it was some years before there was a full translation of the Greek text, the Rosetta Stone enabled academics to finally begin to decipher the hieroglyphic language of ancient Egypt.

Other scientists and doctors that had travelled to Egypt with Napoleon, set up French-style mills, built irrigation systems and established hospitals. The tax system was reformed and local administration was put on a more European footing. In October 1798, Napoleon informed the Directory that, 'All goes perfectly well here; the country is under our control and the people are becoming used to us'.[3] This was, as far as many Arabs saw it, to a large degree quite true, and they gave Napoleon the title of *Sultan El-Adel*, the 'Just Ruler'. But the real rulers of Egypt, the Ottoman Turks, saw things quite differently, and they were determined to evict the invaders. The Ottoman Empire declared war on France.

Siege of Acre

A pincer move was planned at Constantinople, in which the French would be attacked from both land and sea. One arm of the pincer would be formed by the Army of Rhodes, which would be transported by the Royal Navy to land in northern Egypt, while the Army of Damascus advanced through the Sinai. Napoleon, of course, was not the kind of general to sit and allow himself to be attacked in this fashion.

Leaving 10,000 men to hold Egypt, Napoleon aimed to march with the rest of his army across the desert into Palestine, capture the key fortress of Acre, and then defeat the Army of Damascus, before returning to Egypt to meet the amphibious assault from Rhodes. As usual, Napoleon hoped to move quicker than his opponents would expect. With approximately 13,000 men, he set off on the long march through the Sinai, with his heavy artillery transported on two flotillas of naval craft directly across the Mediterranean.

On 6 February 1799, the advance elements of Napoleon's army set off on the long march across the desert. Things began to go wrong from an early date, when they reached the old stone fort of El Arish. The Mameluke-led garrison delayed the French for eleven vital days.

ABOVE: *Jean-Léon Gérôme's portrait of Napoleon in Cairo.* (Princeton University Art Museum)

Finally, on 19 February, the garrison surrendered, and Napoleon moved on rapidly towards Acre, taking Gaza without a shot being fired before reaching Jaffa. There 3,000 Turks retreated into the citadel. It is said that when representatives were sent to demand the surrender of the garrison, they were beheaded and their heads displayed on the city walls. As a result, when Jaffa fell, Napoleon allowed his troops to go on the rampage and he ordered the execution of a large number of the garrison – possibly more than 2,000 men.

After the capture of Jaffa, the French moved up to Acre, arriving before its walls on 20 March. It was expected that Jessar Pasha would soon capitulate. But, supported by a Royal Navy flotilla under the command of Commodore Sir Sidney Smith, the Ottomans defended their city with grim determination. This was helped by Smith intercepting one of the flotillas carrying Napoleon's siege guns; the captured guns were then mounted on the town walls and the French found themselves being fired on by their own guns.

Without the necessary heavy artillery to batter down Acre's huge walls, Napoleon was helpless. After two fruitless months, Napoleon had to give up his expedition and retreat ignominiously back to Cairo. He reached Egypt in time to face the Army of Rhodes at Aboukir. This proved to be his last battle in the Orient, but this, at least, was an overwhelming victory. A month later Napoleon had gone, heading back to France where, once more, the Directory was in trouble and needed its most successful general back in Paris. ❖

ABOVE: *A hand-coloured engraving by Daniel Orme and Robert Cooper showing Rear-Admiral Sir Horatio Nelson, in the centre, during the Battle of the Nile, almost certainly on his flagship, the 74-gun third-rate ship of the line HMS* Vanguard. *Nelson was wounded during the engagement.* (Anne S.K. Brown Military Collection, Brown University Library)

NOTES:
1. In 1795, Britain had seized the Cape of Good Hope, which meant that French ships could not sail round Africa to reach the East.
2. Quoted in A.B. Rodger, *The War of the Second Coalition, 1798-1801* (Clarendon Press, Oxford, 1964), p.20.
3. R.M. Johnston, *In the Words of Napoleon, The Emperor Day by Day* (Frontline, Barnsley, 2015), p.74.

'Not Tonight Joséphine' — Napoleon Bonaparte

ABOVE: *Napoleon's first love, Bernardine Eugénie Clary, who was known as Désirée to her friends.*

Bernardine Eugénie Clary, known as Désirée to her friends, was the sister of Julie Clary who had just married Joseph Bonaparte, Napoleon's elder brother. She was sixteen years old, petite, though still carrying a little puppy fat. She was regarded as good natured, affectionate, 'with a smile like Mediterranean sunshine, and she had large, lustrous, slightly popping brown eyes', and Napoleon wanted to marry her.

The girls were the daughters of François Clary, a wealthy Marseille silk manufacturer and merchant. Their wealth and status probably appealed to the Bonapartes as much as their feminine attractions. It is certainly believed that it was for hard-headed financial reasons that Joseph married Julie. Yet, like so many who had close relationships with Napoleon, the Clary women would reach positions in society they could only ever have dreamed of. (Désirée later married one of Napoleon's marshals, Jean Bernadotte, who became King of Sweden, with Désirée his Queen Consort, and Julie was, for a short time, Queen of Spain – the Bernadottes still remain the Swedish royal family.)

Joseph Bonaparte had followed his father in becoming a lawyer and politician, and was making a name for himself, becoming the Corsican representative in the Council of Ancients, which was the upper house of the French legislature under the Directory. But the Bonaparte brothers were acutely conscious of their Corsican, and therefore immigrant, status, and marrying into a good French family, especially a wealthy one, brought with it the

'Not Tonight Joséphine'
The Women in Napoleon's Life

MAIN PICTURE: *Napoleon and Joséphine making the final preparations for their divorce ceremony on 10 January 1810.*

Napoleon Bonaparte — 'Not Tonight Joséphine'

social respectability they craved. So, after Joseph had married Julie, it only seemed logical for Napoleon to marry the sister. He proposed to her on 21 April 1795.

Doubt has been cast on whether or not Napoleon was love-struck with Désirée, or that he ever really felt strongly enough to have gone ahead with the marriage. Nevertheless, it did his career no harm to be associated in this manner with Désirée, and they certainly became lovers before he was offered command of armée de l'Ouest. When he went to Paris to state his objections to this posting, he threw himself into the social scene, despite the fact that his refusal to take up the position resulted in him being taken off the active list of generals and placed on half-pay.

Though he was evidently on the look-out for a more influential attachment in the metropolis, Napoleon wrote often to Désirée and, on 24 June 1795, he had his portrait painted for her. From his complaints to Joseph that Désirée did not write as frequently, or at length in the manner that he did, it might be the case that neither party was besotted with the other. Indeed, it was Napoleon who admitted to Joseph that he had a 'burning desire to have a home of my own'. But no firm marriage dates were set and, it would appear Désirée had no wish to settle down at that stage in her life.

Meanwhile, Napoleon's head, and his heart, was already being turned by the glamourous women in the French capital. After defending the Directory with his whiff of grapeshot,

he had been reinstated on the list of general officers and his full pay resumed. He now had the money, and the fame, to be taken seriously by the Parisienne elite.

Joséphine De Beauharnais

While it is not known exactly when or where Napoleon first met Désirée, the circumstances surrounding Napoleon's first encounter with Joséphine de Beauharnais have been well recorded. After Napoleon had supressed the revolt against the Directory, he became the talk of Paris and the socialite Joséphine, who had several affairs with the leading politicians of the day, took a fancy to the up and coming young general. Napoleon, who sought acceptance into the Paris elite, saw Joséphine as a suitably influential partner. ▶

'NOT TONIGHT JOSÉPHINE' NAPOLEON BONAPARTE

It was on 15 October that Napoleon visited Joséphine at her house on the rue de Chantereine for the first time. Six years older than Napoleon, having been born on 23 June 1763, and divorced with two children and no private means, it would, on the surface, seem an unlikely liaison. But amongst the politicians she had recently bedded was Paul Barras, the main executive leader of the Directory and one of the most important men in Paris at that time. It would seem that it was Barras who instigated the relationship with Napoleon, effectively handing over his mistress to keep the young general on his side.

Marie Josèphe Rose Tascher de La Pagerie had been born into a wealthy Creole family

ABOVE: *Located on the banks of the Seine in Paris, the Tuileries were badly damaged by fire and explosives on 23 May 1871 (the fires took some time to get under control) and, following the subsequent demolition of the ruins, little of the grand structures remain today. It is the Tuileries garden that can be seen in this image.*
(Lena Ivanova/Shutterstock)

ABOVE: *A portrait of the Empress Joséphine by the artist Andrea Appiani.*

that owned a sugar plantation in Martinique. However, the estate's crops were ruined by a hurricane and a financially-advantageous marriage was arranged for Joséphine with Alexandre, Viscount of Beauharnais. Alexandre Beauharnais was executed during the Reign of Terror, leaving Joséphine to fend for herself and the two children. This she achieved in the time-honoured fashion, soon becoming well known for her voracious sexual appetite. Napoleon fell under her spell and there seems no doubt that he fell genuinely madly in love with her, though her feelings for him were more enigmatic. Nevertheless, they married in March 1796.

Both saw marriage to each other as an opportunity for legitimacy and advancement. But it proved to be a turbulent relationship from almost the outset, and just two days after the marriage, Bonaparte set off to take up his command of the Army of Italy.

At every stop on his way to Nice, Napoleon wrote to his beloved wife. From the tone of his letters, the separation hurt him considerably, whereas Joséphine seemingly took advantage of her husband's absence to carry on enjoying herself.

After his great early success, with much of Italy at his feet, the conqueror called for his wife to join him in Milan. But Joséphine,

ABOVE: *When Napoleon came to power in 1799, he declared that the Tuileries Palace, seen here, would be the official residence of the First Consul and, in due course, the Imperial Palace.*

NAPOLEON BONAPARTE 'NOT TONIGHT JOSÉPHINE'

Joséphine kneels before Napoléon during his coronation at the Notre-Dame Cathedral on 2 December 1804. Behind Napoleon sits Pope Pius VII. The original painting, by Napoleon's official artist, Jacques-Louis David, has imposing dimensions, being almost ten metres across and six metres tall.

Joséphine making her statement of devotion to Napoleon during their divorce ceremony.

who was having an affair with a handsome hussar officer called Hippolyte Charles, merely replied that she was unwell and could not make such a trip.

Napoleon responded by threatening to go to Paris to pick her up himself, with the implied threat that he would march on Paris with his army at his back. This prompted Barras to insist that Joséphine joined her husband, but she took Hippolyte Charles with her amongst her retinue, continuing her affair on the way back to Paris after she had performed her matrimonial duty with General Bonaparte.

A Man Scorned

It was, of course, inevitable that Napoleon would eventually hear of his wife's infidelity, and though he still seems to have loved her, he never trusted her again. As so often the case in such circumstances, Napoleon had no qualms taking lovers himself. Pauline Fourés had dressed as a soldier to accompany her officer husband on the Egyptian expedition. Women had been expressly banned from sailing with the army to the East but many disguised themselves in the way that Pauline did. When Napoleon saw Pauline, he was determined to have her for himself, sending Lieutenant Fourés on a contrived mission. Pauline was soon to be seen frequently with the general and to make sure there were no embarrassing scenes with her husband, Bonaparte arranged for the lieutenant to go back to France.

Fourés set off in the dispatch-boat *Le Chasseur*, but no sooner had it left Alexandria than it was intercepted by the Royal Navy warship HMS *Lion*. The British were well informed of happenings in Cairo and the captain of *Lion* had heard tales of Napoleon's new mistress, so instead of imprisoning Fourés he decided to have some fun and dropped him back at Alexandria.

When Fourés reached Cairo, he learnt that his wife had already settled in with Napoleon. Fourés burst into the palace that the general had taken over, found his wife in the bath, and whipped her severely, until her servants rushed in to help. Though Pauline divorced her husband, Napoleon soon tired of her and he did not take her back with him when he returned to France. ➤

ATTIRE FOR ALL OCCASIONS

When Napoleon became First Consul, he moved into the Tuileries with Joséphine, and she went on a spending spree. She bought 900 dresses a year and 1,000 pairs of gloves. When Napoleon asked his secretary, Louis Bourrienne, to look into his wife's finances, he found a bill for thirty-eight hats in one month alone, along with another bill of 180 francs for feathers to go on the hats. Bourrienne also found a bill for 800 francs worth of perfume (something in the region of £2,225 today). Her total debt amounted to 1,200,000 francs. Napoleon was not pleased. He managed to persuade her debtors to take half of what was owed to avoid a public scandal that might see him driven from office, in which case they would get nothing.

'NOT TONIGHT JOSÉPHINE' NAPOLEON BONAPARTE

ABOVE: *Napoleon presenting his son, Napoléon François Charles Joseph Bonaparte, to French dignitaries, 20 March 1811.*

ABOVE: *A very young looking Napoleon II pictured in the grounds of the Tuileries Palace in Paris.*

When Napoleon's formal marriage request was presented to Marie Louise, she replied, 'I want only what my duty commands me to want'. At 17.30 hours on 11 March 1810, the couple were married. It was hardly a romantic affair, as Marie Louise was still in Vienna and they were married by proxy.

Baby Bonaparte

The newly-weds were soon blessed with a child, Marie Louise giving birth to Napoléon François Charles Joseph Bonaparte on 20 March 1811. Though the marriage was an entirely pragmatic affair, Napoleon does appear to have cared greatly for his wife and she for him.

Napoleon's hopes that a union between France and Austria would mean that he could count on Austria in any subsequent war, however, proved unfounded. The Sixth Coalition against France was formed in March 1813 and although Austria refused to take up arms against Napoleon at the outset, in August of that year, Emperor Francis declared war on France.

When Napoleon was compelled to abdicate in 1814, Marie Louise begged to be allowed to go with him, but he refused, not wishing his son to also become an exile. Instead he asked her to go back to Vienna with the baby Bonaparte so that he could receive a royal upbringing.

Though Napoleon returned to Paris in 1815, he never saw Marie Louise again. With Joséphine having already passed away, as Napoleon marched at the head of his army towards Waterloo, he did so a lonely man. ❖

During his second Italian campaign, Napoleon had an affair with an opera singer called Madame Grazzini, a relationship which ended when he learned that she was also seeing a young violinist from the orchestra.

Despite such dalliances, when Napoleon became Emperor of the French in December 1804, he personally crowned Joséphine as his empress. Their marriage, though, did not last for much longer. It was not just because of her loose morals that Napoleon had become disillusioned with Joséphine. His main disappointment was that she could not produce any more children. Not only was he, being an Italian by blood, desirous of having a large family, but as the Emperor of France he wanted to create a dynasty, and for this he needed an heir.

Despite having been married since 1796, the couple had not produced any offspring. That it was Joséphine with whom the problem lay was made clear to Napoleon in 1809 when, during an affair with a Polish noblewoman, Maria Countess Walewska, a child was born. (The boy, Alexandre Florian Joseph, was accepted by Count Walewska as his own son.)

So, Joséphine had to go.

Outwardly, Joséphine accepted that Napoleon wanted children and that he must find a younger woman, and she partook in an elaborate divorce ceremony on 10 January 1810 in which each read a statement of devotion to the other. Napoleon insisted that she retained the title of empress. She died four years later, on 29 May 1814. The son of her daughter, Hortense, became Napoleon III and, like his step-uncle, Emperor of the French.

The Austrian Princess

Marie Louise (Maria Ludovica Leopoldina Franziska Therese Josepha Lucia), the eldest child of Emperor Francis II of Austria, was just nineteen years old – and she hated the French. She was still a baby when the French Revolution shocked and terrified the monarchies of Europe and she had grown up with her country being in almost continuous conflict with France, and being persistently beaten by Napoleon. Yet she agreed to not only sleep with the enemy but to marry him.

The Austrian princess was not Napoleon's first choice of a replacement for Joséphine. He had earlier approached the Russian Grand Duchess Anne, but had been rebuffed by Czar Alexandre on the grounds that, being only sixteen, she was too young for marriage. So, it was to Austria that he turned.

Being a union between an emperor and a princess, there was much to be negotiated between the two parties. There was also considerable disquiet in Paris and Vienna at the liaison. In the French capital it seemed that Napoleon had abandoned all the principles of the revolution by marrying into one of the families of the *ancien regime* which had so bloodily been removed from French society. Many in France still remembered, and with hatred, Queen Marie Antoinette, another Austrian whom the mob had so despised that they chopped off her head. Napoleon, who had always sought acceptance amongst his social superiors, saw the arrangement as legitimising his own regal status. He also hoped that by marrying into the Austrian royal family it would cement relationships between France and Austria and give him a very powerful ally.

RIGHT: *A portrait of a young Napoleon II.*

LEFT: *Maria Countess Walewska. (Courtesy of Maciej Szczepańczyk)*

VISIT OUR ONLINE SHOP
TO VIEW OUR FULL RANGE OF SPECIAL MAGAZINES ABOUT **HISTORY OF WAR**

Key Shop

shop.keypublishing.com/specials

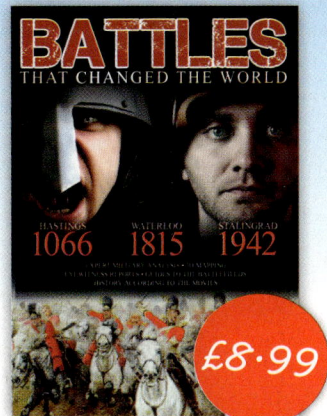 **£8.99**

This 100-page special publication sees Robert Kershaw, one of the UK's leading battle historians, take a unique look at three major battles from world history. Originally released in 2012, Battles That Changed The World is a must-read for anyone with an interest in military history.

 **£8.99**

A reissue of the popular 2019 bookazine. *Hitler's V Weapons*, a 116-page special publication, explores the very moment Allied intelligence first warned of the existence of the V1 and V2 to the full story of the development and operational deployment of these weapons, along with that of the V3.

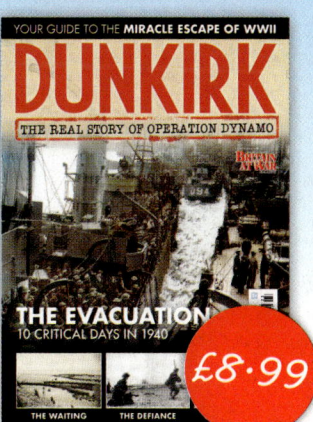 **£8.99**

The story of the great evacuation is told, day-by-day, in this 100-page special publication in the words of those soldiers, sailors and airmen who fought and survived those dramatic nine days in the summer of 1940.

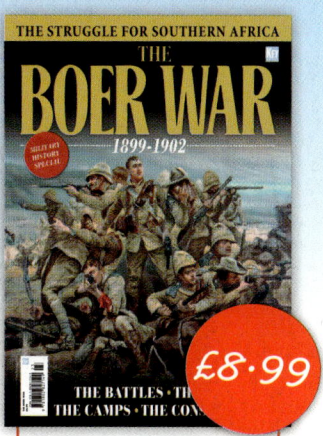 **£8.99**

The Second Boer War was Britain's first modern war, delivering many of the challenges that would dominate World War One and beyond.

It was the birthplace of modern guerrilla warfare, concentration camps, blockhouses, and scorched earth tactics.

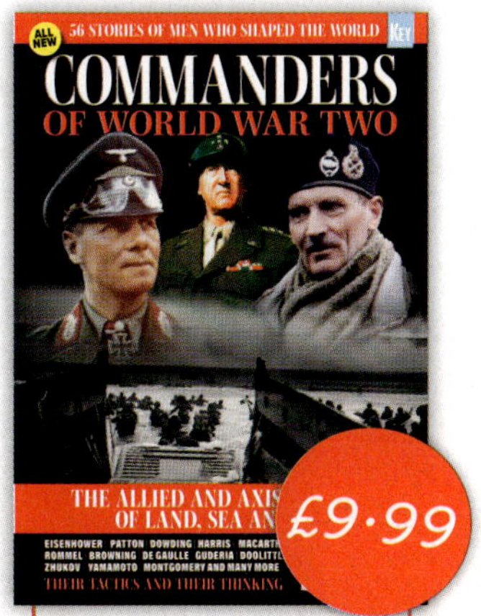

 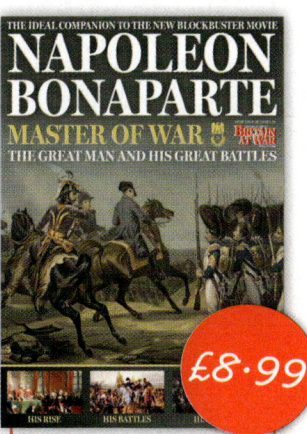 **£9.99** **£8.99**

These are the commanders – the decision makers of World War Two. Their military bearing, bravado, skill, and dedication shaped the outcome of the greatest armed conflict in history. Key Publishing presents a frank and comprehensive overview of these intrepid men and their times.

Napoleon rose from obscure origins in Corsica to become Emperor of the French. The great nations of Europe repeatedly combined their forces against him, only to be thwarted each time by the revolutionary general and his Grande Armée. A reissue of the popular 2018 publication, this expertly researched and illustrated 100-page special provides a real insight into Napoleon Bonaparte – the most powerful man in Europe for more than a decade.

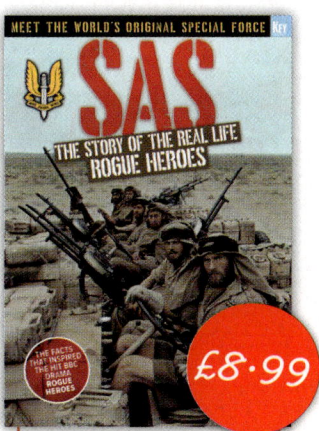 **£8.99**

This special publication has been re-released to celebrate the new BBC drama SAS: Rogue Heroes. It looks back to World War Two and its immediate aftermath to recall the men, the missions and the legends of the force that helped turn the tide against the Axis. Written and researched by renowned special forces expert, Gavin Mortimer.

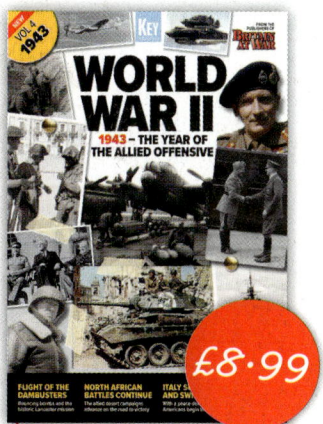 **£8.99**

The year 1943 was crucial in the Allied effort to defeat Axis forces and eliminate German, Italian, and Japanese totalitarian expansionism around the world. Explore the moments that brought Allied triumph inexorably closer and gain greater understanding of the momentous conflict that was World War II.

FREE P&P* when you order online at...
shop.keypublishing.com/specials

Call +44 (0)1780 480404 *(Monday to Friday 9am-5.30pm GMT)*

Also available from **W.H Smith** and all leading newsagents. Or download from **Pocketmags.com** or your native app store - search *Aviation Specials*

SUBSCRIBERS don't forget to use your **£2 OFF DISCOUNT CODE!**

*Free 2nd class P&P on all UK & BFPO orders. Overseas charges apply.

CHARLEMAGNE'S HEIR · NAPOLEON BONAPARTE

MAIN PICTURE: *The famous painting by Jacques Louis David showing Napoleon during the Crossing of the Alps, of which a number of versions exist. Initially begun at the behest of the King of Spain, this oil painting is a highly idealised view of Bonaparte as his army headed through the St Bernard Pass in May 1800. (Library of Congress; LC-USZC4-7159)*

TOP FAR RIGHT: *A British cartoon depicting Napoleon, assisted by a number of grenadiers, driving the members of the Council of Five Hundred from the Orangery at St. Cloud at bayonet point during the coup in November 1799. A drum is labelled 'Vive la Liberté', and papers under foot read 'Resignation des Directoires' and 'Un liste de Membres du Conseil des Cinque Cents'. During what has come to be known as the Coup d'État of Eighteenth Brumaire, Napoleon seized control of the French government and installed himself as First Consul, thereafter governing as a dictator. (Library of Congress; LC-USZC4-6077)*

Charlemagne's Heir

Napoleon I, Emperor of the French

Leaving his army under the command of General Jean-Baptise Kléber, Napoleon set off from Egypt on the frigate *La Muiron* on 23 August 1799, accompanied by just one other frigate. With the Royal Navy in command of the Mediterranean, he was taking an enormous risk, but he managed to slip past Nelson's ships and after forty-seven days at sea, and a quick stop in Corsica (the last time he would ever see his homeland), he reached St Raphael on the Cote d'Azur on 9 October.

When Napoleon had decided to return to France in the summer of 1799, its armies had suffered defeats in Italy, losing almost all the territories won by Napoleon, and had been beaten in Germany and Holland. He had seen these setbacks against the forces of the Second Coalition as his chance to seize power. However, by autumn the situation had been somewhat reversed, with a succession of victories having stabilised the military front.

When Napoleon reached Paris, and assessed the mood in the capital, he had to reconsider his plans. He could no longer ride in as the saviour of France. He also found he was not alone in seeking to take advantage of the unstable political situation caused by the new war against the European monarchies, and he quickly realised that he would have to act with caution.

That the Directory's days were numbered was clear. It had only been able to survive economically through the spoils of war, its army commanders demanding heavy taxes from the countries 'liberated' from the despotic regimes by the forces of the Revolution. Such a policy was unsustainable, and the renewed war had placed increased financial burdens on the government.

As always in times of conflict, with the consequential disruption to agriculture and trade, the prices of most commodities, primarily food, had risen sharply and many everyday items were beyond the reach of the *sans-culottes* – the proletariat of Paris. The only question that remained, was who would take the place of the Directory?

Certainly, Napoleon had much in his favour. Not only was he still a popular general, his brother Lucien had also recently been elected President of the Council of Five Hundred, the lower house of the French legislature. So, Napoleon began to scheme.

First Consul

After much cautious horse-trading, Napoleon had enough support to attempt a coup. On the day of the coup, 9 November (or 18 Brumaire in the Revolutionary calendar), Napoleon assembled the generals who had pledged their support. Lucien, meanwhile, falsely told the two houses of parliament, the Council of Ancients and of Five Hundred, that a Jacobin rebellion was about to break and that they should go to the Palace de Saint-Cloud on the outskirts of Paris and grant General Napoleon ➢

BONAPARTE'S SIBLING

Napoleon's younger brother Lucien (pictured here on the right) had achieved a significant position in French politics as President of the Council of Five Hundred through his own endeavours, not because of any family connection with Napoleon. He was clearly a brilliant individual, and, after Napoleon had cemented his hold on government, Lucien went to Madrid as French Ambassador to Spain, following which he took up the post of senator in the new French government that was formed under Napoleon. Lucien, though, really did believe in the ideals of the Revolution and opposed his brother's imperialist designs.

When Napoleon declared himself emperor, Lucien went into self-imposed exile in Italy. Napoleon exerted pressure on Lucien to return to Paris, virtually placing him under house arrest. Consequently, Lucien tried to escape to the United States but was captured by the Royal Navy and taken to England, where he was allowed to settle, in some comfort, in Worcestershire.

When Napoleon abdicated in 1814, Lucien went back to France, and when Napoleon returned from Elba, Lucien stood by his brother's side once more. He died on 29 June 1840, of stomach cancer, the same disease that claimed his father, his sister Pauline and, as we shall see, his brother Napoleon.

CHARLEMAGNE'S HEIR NAPOLEON BONAPARTE

Having crossed the Alps, the Reserve Army's first battle was at Montebello on 9 June 1800 – the fighting being depicted in this image. (Anne S.K. Brown Military Collection, Brown University Library)

full command of all the troops in the capital and he would protect them. This was agreed and, with all the armed forces in Paris at his disposal, he was in a position to confront the five members of the Directory, forcing three of them to resign. The two others who refused to resign, Louis-Jérôme Gohier and Jean Moulin, were arrested.

They were replaced by a three-member Consulate headed by Napoleon as First Consul. When, the following day, the members of the two councils met at St Cloud, they found the palace surrounded by infantry and cavalry. Upon realising that they had been duped, there was uproar from the rooms where the two Councils were meeting.

Napoleon addressed the Ancients but failed to win them over. He next tried the Five Hundred, but was shouted down, and was even assaulted. At that moment, two of his officers, Murat and Lefebvre, marched in with some of their men and rescued Napoleon. The coup hung in the balance. But then Lucien, laying down his seals as President of the Council of Five Hundred, jumped on a horse and ordered the Guard of the palace forward. At the sight of the advancing bayonets of the Guard, the deputies fled. Napoleon had overturned the government of France, though it was others who had saved the day.

Over the Alps

Having seized power, Napoleon set about restoring France's financial stability. This could only be brought about by peace. But the Austrian aristocracy still wanted to bring down the Revolutionary government in Paris and Britain and refused to discuss peace with France whilst French troops occupied Belgium and Holland.

ABOVE: *Commissioned by Arthur George, 3rd Earl of Onslow, this depiction of Napoleon during the Crossing of the Alps presents an opposing scene to that created by Jacques Louis David.*

Through the wily Talleyrand, Minister of Foreign Affairs, Napoleon tried to find a means to peace, but all such overtures were rejected. The only way peace would be won, it seemed, was on the battlefield.

Being unable to come to grips with the British across the Channel, the First Consul could only hope that by defeating the Austrians the Second Coalition would collapse as the First had done. Once again, it was Italy where Bonaparte was to strike, taking advantage of the fact that General Moreau was mounting a secondary campaign in Germany.

On 18 May 1800, Napoleon led the troops of the so-called Reserve Army over the St

ABOVE: *The imposing Fort Bard, which, along with its garrison, delayed and interrupted Napoleon's forces during their journey over the Alps. The fort was built in the 19th century by the House of Savoy on a rocky prominence above Bard, a town in the Aosta Valley region of north-western Italy.* (Shutterstock)

NAPOLEON BONAPARTE CHARLEMAGNE'S HEIR

TOP: *On 18 May 1803, Britain declared war on France. Napoleon responded by putting forward plans to invade England. This picture shows part of the 200,000-strong Armée d'Angleterre, that was raised as part of this scheme, in camp overlooking the English Channel at Boulogne. (Anne S.K. Brown Military Collection, Brown University Library)*

Bernard Pass. The route was blocked by Fort Bard, which was stoutly defended by the Austrians. In difficult, icy conditions, the French were unable to move their artillery past the fort. At that point, Napoleon took personal charge. By laying straw and dung on the road he was able to bring a few guns quietly past the fort under the cover of darkness. Though later presented as a triumph, the passage of the St Bernard Pass left the French troops almost devoid of artillery or other heavy equipment.

The first battle was fought on 9 June at Montebello, Napoleon's speed, once again, catching the Austrians before they could concentrate their forces. This, though, was a comparatively minor affair, with the decisive clash coming five days later, on 14 June 1800 at Marengo, where Napoleon was attacked by the superior forces of General Melas. The Austrians actually broke through the French line and defeat stared Napoleon in the face, until the sudden arrival of General Desaix's division took the Austrians by surprise and turned defeat into an unlikely victory.

Napoleon, once again, conquered Italy, but it was the great success of Moreau, who achieved a remarkable victory at Hohenlinden in Bavaria, which caused the Austrians to sue for peace, as Moreau's troops bore down on Vienna. Nevertheless, the subsequent Treaty of Lunéville, signed on 9 February 1801, saw most of Italy once again under French control.

Man of Peace

Britain still remained at war with France, but, by this time, the political leaders in London were as desirous of peace as were those in Paris and negotiations led to the Treaty of Amiens. For the first time since the French ➢

LEFT: *The threat of a French invasion was considered so real between 1803 and 1805, that much of the south coast of England was fortified to repel a French landing. As part of the large-scale construction programme, a series of Martello towers were built in Kent and East Sussex, some seventy-four in total. This is Tower 64, which is located at Soveriegn Harbour, Eastbourne, East Sussex. (Michael C. Gray/Shutterstock)*

ABOVE RIGHT: *Napoleon, standing on the beach at Calais, looks out across the English Channel towards the South Coast. (Library of Congress; LC-USZ62-72072)*

CHARLEMAGNE'S HEIR NAPOLEON BONAPARTE

TOP: *A cartoon by James Gillray that shows Napoleon and his army on the seashore after his planned invasion of England, fleeing from the defenders. (Library of Congress; LC-USZ62-111311)*

Revolution had set Europe ablaze, the fire had died down and there was peace amongst the nations. But, it did not last long.

Peace, though, gave Napoleon the chance to rebuild France, both in terms of its administration and its economy. He also brought about a thaw in relationships with the Vatican. Having been de-established during the Revolution, in the Concordat of 1801 with the recently-installed Pope Pius VII, the Roman Catholic Church was reaffirmed as the majority church of France and some of its civil status was restored. This move immediately silenced many royalist groups, who were staunch Catholics. At the same time, Napoleon also relaxed some of the restrictions that had been placed on the émigrés, a number of whom returned to France.

The First Consul then sought to improve France's finances which were in ruins, with, it is said, just 167,000 francs left in the treasury's coffers. Such was his popularity in 1800, having brought peace and reintroduced religion, he was able to impose an additional 25-centime tax and was applauded by the masses for doing so!

By 1801, France was well on the way to recovery and, following further reforms to the tax system, the treasury was able to balance the 1802 budget. Interestingly, the French economy received a boost from the large number of wealthy tourists which thronged to Paris, a place they had been unable to visit for almost ten years.

The First Consul also provided interest-free loans to manufacturers under the agreement that they would take on more workers, and new banks were set up to provide loans for different industries. Little wonder, then, that in August 1802, when Napoleon asked the nation if he should be declared Consul for life, a plebiscite returned 3,600,000 'yes' votes, with only 8,374 'noes'.

The fragile peace was ended by Great Britain (which had become the United Kingdom in 1801), declaring war on France in May 1803.

ABOVE: *Napoleon's coronation ceremony which took place in the Notre Dame Cathedral in Paris on 2 December 1804. By placing the crown on his own head himself, Napoleon was making the gesture that he did not bow to any authority. (Library of Congress)*

BELOW: *As well as new defences throughout the UK, existing sites, such as Dover Castle (seen here), were updated, extended and reinforced. The Army, for its part, also underwent a transformation, leading to a mobilization of the population on a scale not previously attempted in Britain, resulting a combined military force of over 615,000 by December 1803. (Historic Military Press)*

36

NAPOLEON BONAPARTE   CHARLEMAGNE'S HEIR

ABOVE and BELOW: *Despite the fact that Napoleon's invasion plans never came to fruition, the site of his camp at Boulogne was subsequently marked by a fifty-three-metre-high commemorative column topped by a statue of Napoleon. Panels around the base depict Bonaparte presenting the Légion d'Honneur to some of his troops. The Column of the Grande Armée, as it is known, is seen here flanked by its two pavilions at Wimille near Boulogne-sur-Mer.* (Courtesy of Roger Davies)

The reasons for the breach are complex, but principally it was because Britain felt increasingly marginalised in Europe, as well as witnessing a decline in trade with the Continent as Napoleon strengthened his hold over much of Italy. The tipping point seems to have been Napoleon's re-occupation of Switzerland on 19 February 1803, but under the terms of the Treaty of Amiens, Britain was also required to give up Malta, which she had recently taken from the French - a deal she was reluctant to accede to. A fierce diplomatic row ended with war being declared on 18 May.

'If Only Father Could See Us Now!'

Despite the state of war between the two old rivals, there was little prospect of any decisive encounters, for one was a military power and the other a naval one. Certainly, it was Britain, with its global reach, that had more to gain through a resumption of hostilities. France could be certain that its overseas territories would soon be under attack. For his part, Napoleon had to be seen to be doing something – so he decided to invade England!

A vast camp was formed at Boulogne, where the 200,000-strong *Armée d'Angleterre* mustered. Emulating William of Normandy, his men set to work building the armada of boats that would carry them across the Channel.

Napoleon certainly seemed to believe, at least at first, that an invasion of Britain was practical. Certainly, the threat was taken seriously in England where Martello towers and redoubts were erected around the east and southeast coasts, and the enormous engineering project of the Royal Military Canal was taken in hand along the low-lying coast of East Sussex and Kent.

The one obstacle that stood in Napoleon's way, and a formidable one at that, was the Royal Navy. Incredibly, this prompted the idea of using balloons to fly troops over the Channel, which would have marked the first

airborne assault on Britain. Suggestions were also made to dig a tunnel under the Channel. But a more realistic plan was devised to lure the fleets under Nelson and Cornwallis away from the Channel by despatching the French fleet, and that of its ally, Spain, across the Atlantic to the West Indies. When the British ships gave chase, the Franco-Spanish would turn back and protect the invasion flotilla before Nelson and Cornwallis discovered what had happened. 'Let us be masters of the Channel for six hours,' Napoleon declared, 'and we are masters of the world'.

Such sabre-rattling was well-received by the French who had little love for the English. Napoleon was also the target of an assassination plot that was sponsored by the British. When this was brought to light, the French people realised how precarious the existing state of affairs was in France. Few wanted a return to the confusion and corruption of the days of the Revolutionary government. In May 1804, the Senate proposed that Napoleon should be made hereditary emperor. This was put to the people and was confirmed in another plebiscite which yielded an enormous majority in favour.

The coronation took place on Sunday, 2 December 1804, at Notre Dame Cathedral in Paris. Napoleon took the crown from the hands of Pope Pius and placed it on his own head. He then crowned a kneeling Joséphine with a small crown which he had first placed on his own head. The once-despised and bullied Corsican had become the Emperor of France, the first since Charlemagne a thousand years before.

As the emperor and empress were leaving the cathedral Napoleon turned to his brother and exclaimed, 'Ah, Joseph, if only father could see us now!' ❖

THE ARBITER OF VICTORY NAPOLEON BONAPARTE

THE ARBITER OF VICTORY

Napoleon's Imperial Guard: France's Finest Fighting Force

'L a Garde Impériale' was created on 18 May 1804. From its origins as a small personal escort, the Guard grew in size and importance. Eventually, it became both the tactical and strategic reserve of the Grande Armée, compromising almost a third of Napoleon's field forces. The men of the Imperial Guard were the élite of the First Empire, its officers the military aristocracy of post-Revolutionary France. Such was its prestige, that when the attacks of the Guard were repulsed at Waterloo it signalled not only the defeat of the French Army but also the end of an era.

Napoleon's first guard unit was a company of mounted guides allocated to him as commander-in-chief of the Army of Italy in 1796. These men remained part of Napoleon's guard until his final abdication in 1815, and during the years of the Empire, the duty squadrons of Chasseurs were sometimes still referred to as 'guides'. General Bonaparte soon expanded this bodyguard to include two battalions of grenadiers and four companies of mounted guides. The Guides followed Bonaparte to Egypt and 200 returned to France with him in 1799.

On 10 November of that year, when he seized power, it was with the aid of the bayonets of the Grenadiers of the Guard of the Directory. Upon his appointment as First Consul, the Guard of the Directory became known as the Guard of the Consuls. From the very outset, it was intended that the Consular Guard should be a model for the rest of the Army: 'Admission will be restricted to men who have performed heroic actions, have been wounded, or have otherwise given proof ... in several campaigns of their bravery, patriotism, discipline, and exemplary conduct.' ➤

MAIN PICTURE: *Napoleon bids farewell to personnel of the Old Guard, part of the Imperial Guard, in the Cheval-Blanc (White Horse) Courtyard at the Palace of Fontainebleau after his first abdication in 1814.*

NAPOLEON BONAPARTE　　THE ARBITER OF VICTORY

THE ARBITER OF VICTORY NAPOLEON BONAPARTE MASTER OF WAR

ABOVE: An imposing painting of Chasseurs à cheval of the Imperial Guard on campaign in France during 1814. (Anne S.K. Brown Military Collection, Brown University Library)

There were also age restrictions, in that no-one under the age of twenty-five could qualify and candidates had to be between 1.78 and 1.84 metres tall. They had to have served in a minimum of three campaigns and, in the Age of Enlightenment, know how to read and write. The men of the Guard received better pay, clothing, equipment and conditions than the rest of the Army. Each rank in the Guard also rated one step higher than its equivalent in the Line.

After its success at the Battle of Marengo in 1800, the Guard was expanded further, a process that continued up to Napoleon's invasion of Russia twelve years later, when the Guard formed a complete army corps more than 35,000 strong. It then consisted of three infantry divisions, with supporting artillery and engineers, a cavalry division with accompanying horse artillery, and a reserve artillery park. As a whole, the guard eventually itself distinguished between the experienced veterans and less experienced members by being separated into three sections – the Old Guard, Middle Guard and Young Guard.

The Guard at War – The Infantry

The Guard's baptism of fire came at Marengo, a battle so nearly lost by Napoleon. At 13.00 hours on 14 June 1800, the fighting around Marengo had reached a critical point. On the French right, General Ott's Austrians were pouring on to the plain between Castel Ceriolo and Marengo.

On to the plain also marched the Grenadiers and Chasseurs of the Consular Guard. Formed in square, the Guard – less than 1,000 men – stood firm as the Austrian cavalry swept towards them across the plain. Ott's advance was halted. The Austrians brought forward their artillery and pounded the exposed square. But the Guard's discipline held, and Ott was forced to re-group, before renewing his assault on the weakened French positions around Marengo. The Guard had bought Bonaparte time to bring up reinforcements, and for the First Consul to win the lost battle. The Guard had endured a terrible bombardment but had never wavered. The Guard's reputation for invincibility had been created.

Five years were to pass before the Guard marched into battle once more and then, at Austerlitz in 1805, it was the cavalry which was to win most of the glory. The Guard infantry formed the reserve. It was only committed to the fray when the Pratzen Heights – the tactical high ground – were in French hands and the battle effectively won.

This was to be the role of the Guard in Napoleon's future battles. This body of experienced, disciplined and highly motivated troops was to be held in reserve to form the spearhead of the *masse de decision*, the ones who would deliver the final, decisive blow. They would become the arbiters of victory.

This, though, meant that they would only be used sparingly, and so it was a year later at Jena. The Guard stood in reserve, and there it remained throughout the battle as Napoleon defeated the Prussians without the aid of his élite. At Eylau in 1807, the battalions of the Guard were spectators throughout much of the battle. In Napoleon's eyes, the Guard had become 'so precious one fears to expose them'.

At the decisive Battle of Wagram in 1809, the Guard infantry, including the recently created Young Guard regiments, formed a massive central reserve. It nearly cost him the battle. Eventually, though, he had to commit most of his precious Guard to secure victory.

It was argued that the existence of such a corps d'élite reduced the fighting capabilities of the rest the army. This was because the best men from each regiment were continually being drafted into the Guard. But the presence of such a potent force as the Guard allowed Napoleon to commit all his other troops into battle without fearing for his own security or that of the rear of the army.

ABOVE: Chasseurs à cheval of the Imperial Guard depicted charging at the Battle of Austerlitz, where they delivered the first of their many famous and daring charges. (Anne S.K. Brown Military Collection, Brown University Library)

ABOVE: Napoleon giving his battle orders to mounted staff officers during the Battle of Austerlitz, 2 December 1805. (Anne S.K. Brown Military Collection, Brown University Library)

Napoleon may have been justified in keeping the Guard in hand in his earlier battles, but at Borodino in 1812 his determination to preserve his Guard infantry cost him the campaign. When asked by his Marshals to release the Guard at the critical stage of the battle, he retorted with the words, 'And if there should be another battle tomorrow, where will be my army to fight it?' Napoleon therefore preserved his Guard only to lose it in the disastrous winter retreat from Moscow. More than 20,000 strong at Borodino, the Guard was reduced to less than 2,000 when it crossed the Elbe just six months later.

The irony of saving his guard in battle only for it to be wasted on the march was not lost

Napoleon Bonaparte — The Arbiter of Victory

ABOVE: *The Battle of Lützen unfolding on 2 May 1813. Napoleon and other mounted officers can be seen in the foreground.* (Anne S.K. Brown Military Collection, Brown University Library)

on Napoleon. In his next major engagement, at Lützen on 2 May 1813, the Guard was to play a decisive role. The critical moment of the battle came at 18.00 hours when Napoleon launched his grand attack upon the Allied centre. The attack was preceded by seventy guns of the Guard followed by the Young Guard formed into four columns, each consisting of four battalions, with the Old Guard, the most senior regiments of the army, and the Guard cavalry in support. The Guard drove the entire Allied line back in disorder, clinching a notable victory for the Emperor.

Possibly the most famous attack delivered by the Guard was its last. This occurred, perhaps predictably, at Waterloo. The climax of the battle was reached when Napoleon led the 3rd and 4th Grenadiers and Chasseurs against Wellington's Anglo-Allied line. Apart from two batteries of Artillerie à Cheval, the attack of these seven battalions was almost unsupported. Assailed in front and on their flanks by the Allied artillery, the Guards were severely weakened as they mounted the Mont St John. The Grenadiers were halted by the Allied artillery, whilst the Chasseurs were caught in a semi-circle of fire from the British Guards Brigade and the 52nd Light Infantry. The Allies then charged the shaken columns and the Guards, having lost their momentum, were driven back down the ridge.

With the repulse of the Guard, the French army disintegrated. Napoleon used his remaining four battalions of the Old Guard to try and stop the fleeing troops, but to no avail, they did, though slow the Allied pursuit temporarily. Though surrounded by enemy cavalry and their ranks decimated by the Allied artillery, the Old Guard retired in good order with its drums still beating. ➢

ABOVE: *Chasseurs à cheval of the Imperial Guard depicted whilst on campaign in Spain, 1808.* (Anne S.K. Brown Military Collection, Brown University Library)

ABOVE: *Part of an unfinished panorama of the Battle of Somosierra, this is entitled 'The Charge'. Napoleon's victory in the Pass cleared the last obstacle barring the road to Madrid.*

THE ARBITER OF VICTORY · NAPOLEON BONAPARTE MASTER OF WAR

A depiction of the Battle of Somosierra, 30 November 1808.

The Guard At War – The Cavalry

As with the infantry, the Guard cavalry fought at Marengo, but it was at Austerlitz that it delivered the first of its many famous and daring charges. The key to the battlefield of Austerlitz was the Pratzen Heights. The heights had been stormed by the Russian Imperial Guard and the struggle for this crucial high ground hung in the balance. Against the Russian elite, Napoleon sent his Guard cavalry. With four guns of the Artillerie à Cheval galloping ahead, two squadrons of the Chasseurs à Cheval and the Mamelukes of the Guard and they threw them back, inflicting more than 500 casualties. But the Chasseurs were stopped by the fresh squadrons of the Russian Guard cavalry and in response Napoleon ordered the Grenadiers à Cheval to clear the heights. The Grenadiers tipped the balance, the heights were secured, and the Battle of Austerlitz was all but won.

The Guard had no part to play in the twin victories of Jena-Auerstadt, but at Eylau the Grenadiers and Chasseurs à Cheval again charged to glory. At an early stage in the battle Napoleon was compelled to commit his cavalry reserve into the fray to save his weakened centre. Murat's line cavalry, eighty magnificent squadrons, punched through the Russian line, reformed, and charged back through the enemy positions. As the Russians tried to restore their shattered ranks, Napoleon released his Guard cavalry to inflict further damage upon the Russians and to aid Murat's now exhausted troopers. On this occasion, the Grenadiers led the charge of the French cavalry. This not only relieved the pressure on Napoleon's centre but also forced a hole in the Russian line. Had the Emperor been prepared to expose his infantry of the Guard, it could have resulted in the victory Napoleon sought instead of the frustratingly inconclusive result.

The early period of the Peninsular War saw one memorable charge by the cavalry of the Guard. As the French marched towards Madrid the Spaniards undertook a desperate attempt to halt the invaders at the Somosierra

ABOVE: *Men of the duty squadron of the 1er Régiment de Chevau-Légers Polonais, part of the Imperial Guard, in action during the Battle of Somosierra.* (Anne S.K. Brown Military Collection, Brown University Library)

Napoleon accepts the surrender of Madrid on 4 December 1808 – a consequence of his victory a few days earlier at the Somosierra Pass.

Napoleon Bonaparte — The Arbiter of Victory

driven back, with only twenty-eight men left in the saddle. The next attack was a properly coordinated assault, with French infantry on either side of the road. The remaining two squadrons of the Chevaux-Lèger, supported by the Chasseurs à Cheval, charged up the road and finally took the pass with little further loss.

Napoleon used the Guard cavalry as a highly mobile reserve either to support the Guard infantry and exploit any breakthrough they might have achieved, or to seize a tactical objective. At Lützen and Bautzen in 1813, and Montmiral in 1814, the Guard à cheval and à pied together delivered the decisive attacks that won the day.

Napoleon was always far more willing to use his Old Guard cavalry than his Old Guard infantry. At Waterloo he allowed the cavalry to be thrown prematurely against the British squares. When the infantry made its fateful attack against Wellington's line, Napoleon had no formed cavalry left to support it.

The Artillery

'In battle,' wrote Napoleon, 'the Guard furnishes artillery to the whole field'. Of all the Guard regiments, it was the artillery which became Napoleon's most effective weapon. The Emperor, more than any other commander of his day, was conscious of the power of massed artillery and he always attempted to keep his Guard artillery concentrated for maximum effect.

At Austerlitz in 1805, the Guard artillery stabilised a dangerous situation when it rushed forward with twenty-four guns to fill a gap in the French line, and from that battle onwards the Guard artillery became concentrated in ever greater numbers. At Jena, a year later, Napoleon kept all the Guard artillery under his own hand, ready to move at a moment's notice to decide the outcome of the battle. As it happened, the battle was won without the necessity of the Guard's involvement but it clearly indicated the direction in which Napoleon's tactics were heading.

ABOVE: *Officers and men of the Grenadiers à Cheval of the Imperial Guard circa 1813.* (Anne S.K. Brown Military Collection, Brown University Library)

Pass some sixty miles north of the capital. The pass was defended by 9,000 men and sixteen guns positioned behind a hastily-constructed earthwork. Napoleon sent forward a division of infantry to clear the pass. However, their progress was too slow for the Emperor and he ordered his duty squadron of the 1er Régiment de Chevau-Légers Polonais to take the pass at the gallop.

Consisting of just seven officers and eighty-one men, the Polish Light Horse formed up four abreast across the narrow road and charged straight towards the Spanish position. The first salvos from the Spanish cannon brought the Poles to a halt, but Napoleon ordered them forward again. This time they almost reached the enemy positions before they were

Napoleon watches a parade by Chasseurs à Cheval of the Imperial Guard near the Tuileries Palace, 1810. (US Library of Congress; LC-DIG-pga-0312)

BELOW: *Chasseurs à Cheval of the Imperial Guard charging Austrian dragoons at the Battle of Wagram, 5–6 July 1809.*

THE ARBITER OF VICTORY　NAPOLEON BONAPARTE MASTER OF WAR

This was demonstrated in 1809 at Wagram, where the massed batteries of the Guard played a crucial role in the battle. On the second day of the battle, Napoleon found himself under attack and he had to rearrange his troops to meet this unexpected emergency. In the re-deployment of the various French Corps, a large gap developed in the very centre of the French line. The reserve cavalry bought valuable time by repeatedly charging the advancing Austrians. This allowed Napoleon to call up the seventy-two guns of the Guard artillery. Combined with forty guns from Eugene's corps, they formed a massive battery of 112 pieces. Placed under the command of General Lauriston, the guns halted the Austrian attack and then, in turn, switched onto the offensive. The Artillerie à Cheval of the Guard was posted on the flanks, with the heavy 12-pounders of the Artillerie à Pied in the centre. The great battery – stretching over a mile in length – successfully drove the Austrians back from all their forward positions.

At Borodino in 1812, the opposing French and Russian armies had at their disposal very large numbers of cannon. The French had 587 assorted pieces and the Russians approximately 640 guns, of which almost a quarter were 12-pounders. Both commanders adopted similar tactical dispositions. Napoleon drew up 120 guns in battery with the Guard artillery forming the reserve. Kutuzov had eighteen 12-pounders sited in a large redoubt at the heart of the Russian defence, with a further thirty-eight in battery in earthworks on the flanks and another 150 pieces scattered along the Russian front. Twenty-six batteries, totalling nearly 300 pieces, were held in reserve to the rear to the south.

Napoleon chose to direct his main thrust against the thinly-held Russian flank from the redoubt southwards. The French attack was preceded by a fierce bombardment from

ABOVE: *A stylized depiction of the final moments of the Old Guard at Waterloo.* (Anne S.K. Brown Military Collection, Brown University Library)

ABOVE: *The Old Guard in action during their last stand at Waterloo, 18 June 1815.* (Anne S.K. Brown Military Collection, Brown University Library)

ABOVE: *General Antoine, comte Drouot, commanded the entire Imperial Guard at Waterloo.* (Anne S.K. Brown Military Collection, Brown University Library)

the front-line batteries of both armies. Led by marshals Ney and Murat, the French attack met stubborn resistance, but gradually the Russian's left wing was pushed back. Kutuzov's generals responded by despatching Tolstoy's Corps from the north, which Napoleon countered by releasing the sixty guns of the Guard artillery.

Shielded by Murat's cavalry, the Guard unlimbered in the centre of the Russian positions and with roundshot and then canister they decimated Tolstoy's Corps as it tried to advance. This enabled the Guard to turn its guns on the redoubt which then became the focal point of the French attack. General Kutaisov, the Russian artillery commander, ordered forward some of the reserve cannon until 300 guns were in action along this sector of the battlefield. But at this stage of the battle Kutaisov was killed and the movement of guns from the rear came to a halt. The French attacked the redoubt repeatedly, aided by the fire of 170 guns, and the position eventually fell to the attackers, piercing the Russian centre. Had Napoleon launched his Guard infantry into the battle at that point he might have won a decisive victory, but instead the Russians were able to retreat largely intact.

Following the disastrous retreat from Moscow, Napoleon was increasingly forced to depend upon the Guard artillery to support the raw recruits of the new armies he had to raise. The Guard artillery was expanded and furnished with more of the heavier ordnance – the 12-pounder cannon and the 8-inch howitzers – which was used to blast holes in the enemy lines. At Lützen, seventy guns of the Guard were initially used defensively to halt the Allied attack and then offensively as they led the successful French counter-attack. At Dresden and Leipzig, the artillery was again used as an offensive weapon, advancing against the enemy positions. At Hanau, the guns of the Guard were used to clear a path for the retreating French army, and at Ligny in 1815, sixty guns supported the attack of the Guard infantry that destroyed the Prussian centre.

Such success led Napoleon to claim, 'It is the artillery of my Guard which decides my battles, for, as I have it always at hand, I can bring it to bear whenever it becomes necessary.' Napoleon's enemies were never quite able to emulate his bold handling of massed artillery, but they fully appreciated its effects and on numerous occasions the Allies fought with more guns than the French. As Field Marshal Blücher once observed, 'Against Napoleon you needed guns – and lots of them!' ❖

Napoleon during the Battle of Jena-Auerstadt, which is featured by Robert Burnham on pages 50 and 51. (Anne S.K. Brown Military Collection, Brown University Library)

NAPOLEON'S GREATEST BATTLES

Introduced and selected by historian and author Robert Burnham, the following gallery of paintings and prints details five battles that defined Napoleon.

Napoleon fought sixty battles, losing only eight, four of which were after his disastrous Russian campaign. Which of those battles could be regarded as his 'greatest' victories is hard to determine, and must be considered largely subjective.

This is particularly the case with the Battle of Ulm in 1805, in which an entire Austrian army was compelled to surrender without a major engagement. The Austrians, under General Mack, were surrounded by Napoleon's various corps and cut off from the other forces marching to join them. For the loss of just 500 men killed, Napoleon captured 27,000 men and sixty-six artillery pieces, in what is widely regarded as one of his finest strategic operations, yet in terms of actual fighting, scarcely merits the term 'battle'.

For his part, Napoleon himself is alleged to have remarked that the series of manoeuvres that culminated in the defeat of the Austrians at Eckmühl in 1809 as 'the finest' that he ever conducted. In this campaign, Napoleon was taken by surprise when the Austrians launched a pre-emptive strike on his forces in Germany.

However, in what has become known as the Landshut Manoeuvre, he regained the initiative by holding the Austrians with part of his army whilst he attempted to swing round with the rest of his force onto the rear of the enemy.

Napoleon employed this *manoeuvre de derrière* frequently in his battles, and usually with success. This was only achievable because of the corps system which he had developed. In what is today regarded as standard military practice, but which at the start of the nineteenth century was unusual, each of his corps was an army in miniature, complete with infantry, cavalry, artillery and support services. Each corps could operate independently of the main body of the army and could hold off attacks (for a limited time) from much larger forces. One corps could, therefore, hold down the enemy whilst Napoleon moved the bulk of his army round his opponent's flank, causing chaos and confusion in the enemy's ranks.

Though any number of Napoleon's battles could have been selected by the historian and author Robert Burnham as being his 'greatest', the following are certainly amongst his finest victories.

Robert Burnham hosts the pre-eminent Napoleonic website, the *Napoleon Series*. This fascinating and all-embracing website is a 'must' for anyone interested in the Napoleonic era. It can be found at: **www.napoleon-series.org**

NAPOLEON'S GREATEST BATTLES — NAPOLEON BONAPARTE

1. Marengo (14 June 1800)

NAPOLEON CONSIDERED Marengo as one of his greatest victories, second only to Austerlitz. Faced by multiple enemies, including Great Britain, Austria, and Russia, Napoleon went to the rich agricultural areas of northern Italy to deal with the biggest threat – an Austrian army that was advancing towards France.

Napoleon crossed the Alps in May 1800 and caught the Austrians by surprise. On 14 June, Napoleon, with an army of 24,000 men and twenty-four guns, faced the Austrians under General Michael von Melas, who had 31,000 men and 100 guns. The Austrians attacked the French centre and after several hours of intense fighting, the French began to fall back.

The timely arrival of French reinforcements allowed them to hold, but the situation continued to deteriorate. By 17.00 hours the Austrian commander had left the battlefield thinking the French were defeated.

Soon after he left, however, more French troops arrived and turned a likely French defeat into a disaster for the Austrians. A

MAIN PICTURE: *Bataille de Marengo, an oil on canvas by Louis-François Lejeune.*
RIGHT: *The memorial commemorating the battle that can be seen in Marengo.* (Courtesy of Szeder László)

Napoleon Bonaparte — Napoleon's Greatest Battles

cavalry charge shattered the Austrian right flank and their army began to disintegrate. Their assured victory quickly turned into a massive rout. By the end of the night fifty percent of the Austrian army had been killed, wounded, or taken prisoner.

Over the next fifteen years, Napoleon would inspire his troops before a battle by evoking the memory of Marengo as an example of what French soldiers could achieve if they tried hard enough.

RIGHT: *Napoleon, on the white horse, and his aides at the Battle of Marengo.* (Anne S.K. Brown Military Collection, Brown University Library)

Napoleon's Greatest Battles — Napoleon Bonaparte

2. Austerlitz (2 December 1805)

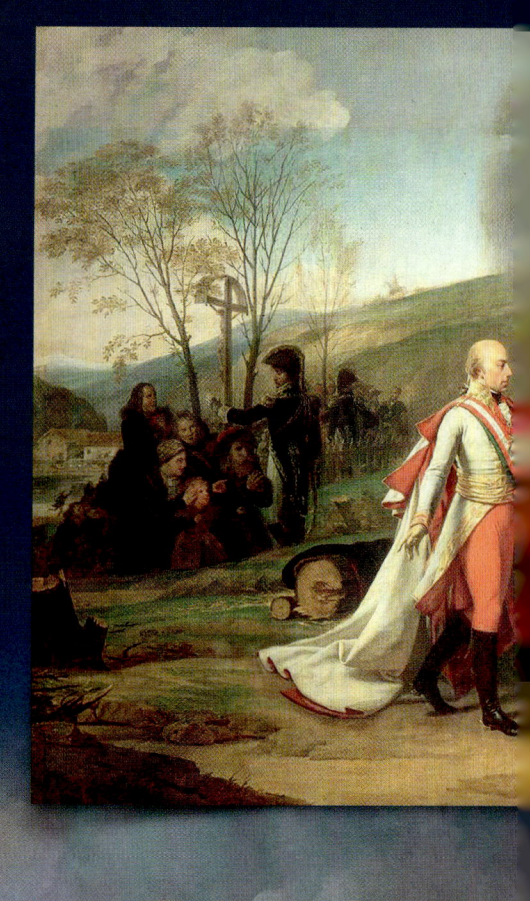

IN MARCH 1802 peace had finally come to Europe. It did not last long. In December 1804, Great Britain, Austria, and Russia declared war on France. Whilst Napoleon originally planned to invade England, the mobilization of the Russians and Austrians, however, compelled him to turn his attention eastward.

By mid-November he had forced the main Austrian army to surrender and had captured Vienna. On 2 December he met the Russians and a small Austrian force 150 kilometres north of Vienna at Austerlitz. Napoleon deployed his 70,000 men and 142 guns on the plains below the Pratzen Heights. On the heights was an Allied army of 82,000 men and 323 guns.

Napoleon deliberately weakened his right flank, hoping they would move against it. About 08.00 hours, the Allies took the bait and attacked it with a large portion of their army. Once they were committed to the attack, Napoleon counter-attacked in the centre with the bulk of his army and by 14.00 hours had split the Allied army in two. He then shifted his forces from there and hit the Allies who were attacking on his right.

By dusk the Allied army was shattered and its remnants were retreating east. The French had less than 9,000 casualties while the Allies lost 30,000 men and 197 guns. Napoleon's victory was total, and the Austrians sued for peace on 24 December. The Russians were permitted to return home. Napoleon considered Austerlitz his greatest victory and historians often use it as an example of his military genius.

Napoleon Bonaparte — Napoleon's Greatest Battles

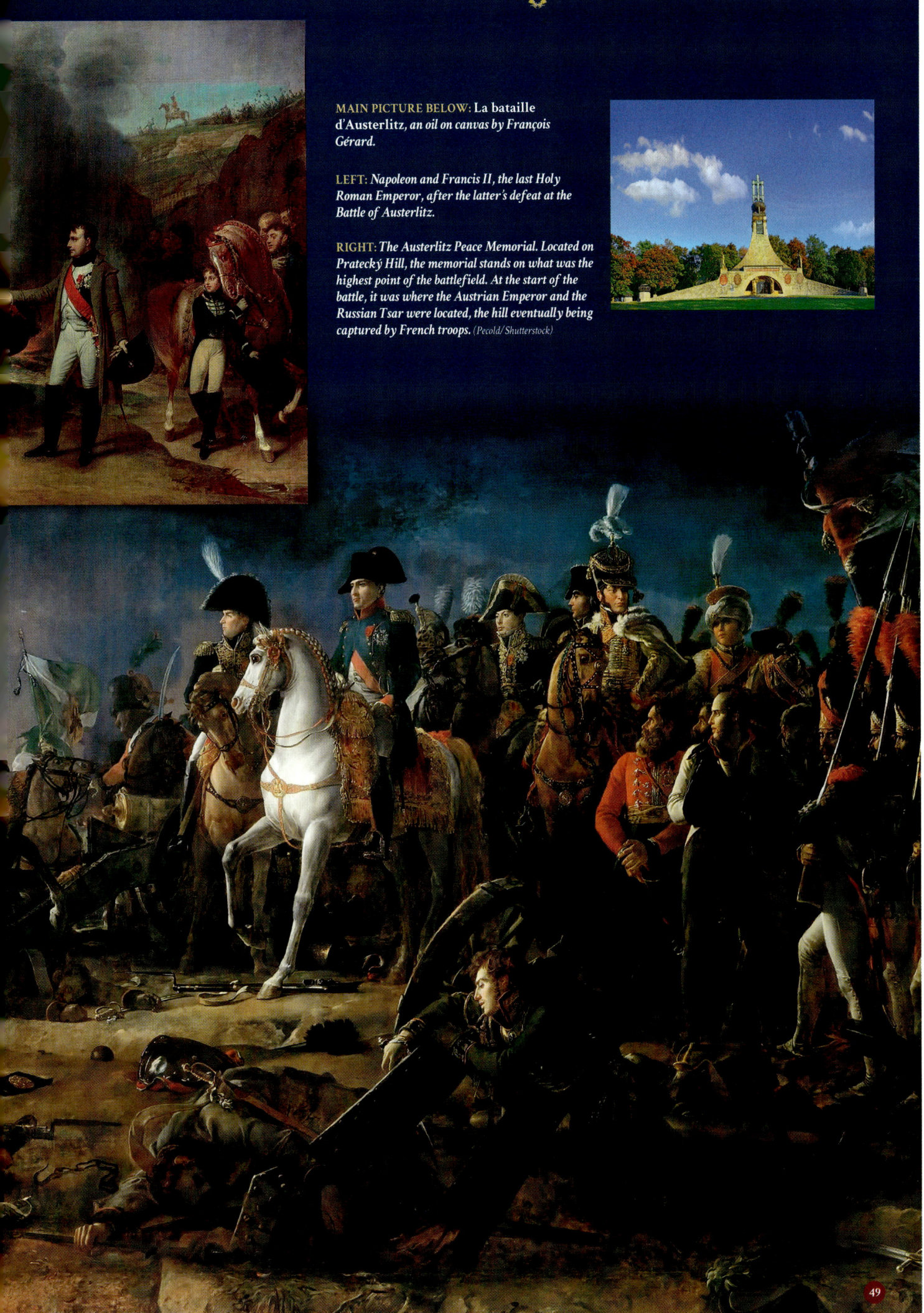

MAIN PICTURE BELOW: *La bataille d'Austerlitz*, an oil on canvas by François Gérard.

LEFT: *Napoleon and Francis II, the last Holy Roman Emperor, after the latter's defeat at the Battle of Austerlitz.*

RIGHT: *The Austerlitz Peace Memorial. Located on Pratecký Hill, the memorial stands on what was the highest point of the battlefield. At the start of the battle, it was where the Austrian Emperor and the Russian Tsar were located, the hill eventually being captured by French troops.* (Pecold/Shutterstock)

Napoleon's Greatest Battles | Napoleon Bonaparte

3. Jena-Auerstadt (14 October 1806)

AFTER DEFEATING the Austrian and Russian armies at Austerlitz on 2 December 1805, Napoleon was the dominant power in Germany. However, his plans to reorganize the political structure of Germany were opposed by Prussia.

The situation deteriorated through much of 1806 and by August, the Prussians began mobilizing their army. In early October Napoleon launched a pre-emptive strike with his 125,000-man army. The 120,000-strong Prussian Army was divided into two wings, each of about 60,000 men.

The two armies met on 14 October in what is known as the Battle of Jena-Auerstadt. Napoleon and 90,000 men fought

The famous Pont d'Iéna in Paris was built to commemorate the Battle of Jena, its construction being ordered by Napoleon in 1807. (Shutterstock)

Napoleon Bonaparte Napoleon's Greatest Battles

the southern wing of the Prussian Army at Jena. Thirty-five kilometres to the north, at Auerstadt, Marshal Davout with 25,000 men fought the other wing. In five hours, Napoleon and Davout had crushed the Prussian Army. Twenty thousand Prussians were killed or wounded, another 18,000 taken prisoner, and over 230 guns captured. The French casualties were less than 7,000.

The subsequent pursuit of the demoralized Prussian Army was the most brilliant feat of arms Napoleon and his army ever achieved. Over the next month, the French army systematically surrounded and captured tens of thousands of troops and forced all of Prussia's fortresses to capitulate.

On 25 October, Marshal Davout marched his victorious troops through Berlin. By 11 November only a small force of Prussians still remained in the field. The Prussians were militarily destroyed. Their loss of territory and harsh reparations imposed ensured that they would be no threat to Napoleon until 1813.

ABOVE: *Napoleon's victorious entry into Berlin on 27 October 1806.*

MAIN PICTURE BELOW: Bataille d'Jéna, *a contemporary hand-coloured copper-engraving.*
(Anne S.K. Brown Military Collection, Brown University Library)

NAPOLEON'S GREATEST BATTLES ✦ NAPOLEON BONAPARTE

4. Friedland (14 June 1807)

AFTER DESTROYING the Prussian army in the autumn of 1806, Napoleon and his forces continued east in an attempt to finish matters with the Russians. To counter these moves, the Russians made a surprise attack in January and caught the French army unprepared.

A battle was fought on 7 and 8 February at Eylau. At the end of the second day of fighting, both sides, having taken heavy casualties, withdrew and went into winter quarters.

Hostilities began again in May and by 13 June, Napoleon's advance guard caught the 60,000-man Russian army under the command of General Bennigsen on the west bank of the Alle River at the town of Friedland. Although initially outnumbered, the French, under Marshal Jean Lannes, held on until Napoleon and reinforcements began arriving around noon. For the next five hours the French were on the defensive.

At 17.00 hours Napoleon felt that he had worn the

MAIN PICTURE BELOW: *Friedland, 1807, an oil on canvas by Ernest Meissonier.*

ABOVE RIGHT: *A drawing depicting the auction in New York during which the original of Meissonier's Friedland, 1807 sold for what was then the astonishing sum of $66,000. (Everett Historical/Shutterstock)*

Russians down and ordered his army, whose strength was now at 80,000 men, to attack. A heavy artillery bombardment at close range, followed by a massive infantry attack, broke the Russians. They unsuccessfully tried to retreat to safety across the river.

French casualties were about 10,000, while the Russians lost 20,000 men and eighty artillery pieces. The Russians were forced to ask for an armistice. The subsequent Treaty of Tilsit saw the dismemberment of much of Prussia and fixed the eastern boundary of Napoleon's Empire at the Vistula River. Russia and France would be at peace for the next five years.

RIGHT: *Napoleon at the Battle of Friedland. He is depicted giving instructions to General Oudinot. Between them is General de Nansouty, whilst behind the Emperor, on his right, is Marshal Ney.*

5. Wagram (5–6 July 1809)

NAPOLEON'S SECOND largest battle was that at Wagram, which was fought on 5-6 July 1809. Austria was not happy with the terms imposed on it after losing the war with Napoleon in 1805.

In April 1809, hoping to regain the political and economic dominance over central Europe that it lost four years before, Austria invaded Bavaria, Poland, and Italy, which were French allies or protectorates. Napoleon was unprepared for war and the Austrians initially made enormous gains. After a series of defeats in late April the Austrians retreated to Austrian territory and then across the Danube River. Wishing to finish the war quickly Napoleon crossed the Danube on 21 May, but suffered his first defeat in nine years at the battle of Aspern-Essling.

LEFT: *Napoleon in conference with his senior generals late on 5 July, after the first day of battle.*

NAPOLEON BONAPARTE | NAPOLEON'S GREATEST BATTLES

On 6 July he crossed the river a second time with 150,000 men. He met the 158,000-strong Austrian army, commanded by Archduke Charles, at the village of Wagram, where a battle ensued.

The first day saw heavy casualties on both sides, but the French were able to out-manoeuvre the Austrians the next day and forced them to retreat. After being defeated at Znaim on 10-11 July, the Austrians sued for peace. This campaign was the last in which Napoleon decisively defeated his opponent and was thus able to dictate terms.

Austria became Napoleon's reluctant ally for the next four years. As part of the arrangement, the Austrian Emperor had to agree to Napoleon marrying his eighteen-year-old daughter, Princess Marie Louise.

MAIN PICTURE: *This water colour by Horace Vernet depicts Napoleon directing his forces during the Battle of Wagram.*
(Anne S.K. Brown Military Collection, Brown University Library)

THE LEGION D'HONNÉUR ✦ NAPOLEON BONAPARTE

THE LEGION D'HONNÉUR

'It is with baubles that men are led'

The Revolution that swept away the *Ancien Régime* had taken with it many of the traditions and customs which had become integral to French life. The disestablishment of the Roman Catholic Church had also left a moral void and the determination to depose the despised aristocrats at all costs had seen the removal of the ancient honorific codes. The awarding of honours and titles for outstanding service to the state, unrelated to any financial reward, has always had widespread appeal. Recognition of an individual's contribution to the betterment of his fellows, unsullied by motives of profit, is a powerful incentive recognised by all regimes.

Napoleon felt that there was a need to reintroduce some system of honouring merit, available to all classes in society, military and civilian, that would help bring the French people together around a common ideal of individual and national honour. This would, he hoped, combine the courage of the soldiers and sailors with the creativity of the civilians. This would, by its very nature, create a new elite and, in opposition to the principles of the Revolution, raise one man above the

ABOVE LEFT: *Standing at the top of a triple-tiered platform, Napoleon presents the Légion d'Honneur to a veteran who lost a foot during battle.* (Library of Congress; LC-USZ62-128801)
ABOVE RIGHT: *As Emperor, Napoleon always wore the Cross and Grand Eagle of the Légion d'Honneur.* (Library of Congress; LC-P87-119x)

ABOVE: *Located on the Left Bank of the River Seine in Paris, the Palais de la Légion d'Honneur, also known as the Hôtel de Salm, is the seat of the Légion d'Honneur, the highest French order of merit. It also houses the Musée de la Légion d'Honneur. Constructed between 1782 and 1787, the building was nationalised by the revolutionary government, taking on its role as the seat of the Légion d'Honneur on 13 May 1804.* (Lena Ivanova/Shutterstock)

other. But Napoleon sought to create not an aristocracy, but a meritocracy. Only this way, he felt could the talents and enterprise of the French people be unleashed.

When he presented his ideas for a new award to the *Conseil d'État*, the Council of State, one of the members of the council questioned the value of such 'baubles'. To this Napoleon replied:

'You call these baubles, well, it is with baubles that men are led … Do you think that you would be able to make men fight by reasoning? Never. That is only good for the scholar in his study. The soldier needs glory, distinctions, and rewards.

'I do not think that the French love liberty and equality; they have not been changed by ten years of revolution; they are what the Gauls were, fierce and fickle. They are accessible to only one sentiment, the love of honour. That is why we must have distinctions … Soldiers must

Napoleon Bonaparte — The Legion D'honnéur

MAIN PICTURE: *Napoleon presides over the first investitures of the Légion d'Honneur at Les Invalides, 14 July 1804.*

be allured by fame and pay… Here is a new kind of money assessed at a different valuation from current coin. Its source is inexhaustible. With no other kind of money, is it possible to reward actions which are so sublime that they cannot be valued in current coin.'[1]

On 19 May 1802, the founding of the new honour was approved by fifty-six votes to thirty-eight in the Tribunat and 166 votes to 110 in the Corps Législatif. The new honour, the First Consul said, would be a reward, 'for outstanding merit acquired in the service of the nation in a civilian or military capacity'. It was to be called the *Legion d'Honneur* and, despite Napoleon's views that the French were not interested in equality, the new honour was truly egalitarian, in that there would be, 'no privileges, no exemptions, no remuneration, but the recognition only of individual merit, acquired and not transmitted'.

From the beginning, Napoleon decorated 'his soldiers and his savants', choosing from Marshals of the Empire and veterans of the Revolutionary Wars, as well as senior civil servants, judges, doctors, industrialists, scientists, artists, architects, musicians, and writers. Though Napoleon decorated both soldiers and civilians, the First Consul owed his position to the Army, and in the early distribution of the *Legion d'Honneur* military personnel accounted for about 75 per cent of the total.

Often the medal was presented by Bonaparte himself, although the more usual way for a soldier to get the coveted recognition was via his senior regimental officer who would be told the number of new legionnaires to be created and then picked the men himself. The Legion also ran a hospital for its members.

Then, in 1807 Napoleon took a controversial step which, in the eyes of many, went against all the principles behind the creation of the *Legion d'Honneur* – he made it hereditary. No longer would sacrifice or ability be the sole factors in determining the membership of the Legion, but also birth right. This was nothing but a return to the days of the old hereditary aristocracy, the very thing that had caused the Revolution.

But much had already changed since 1802. The First Consul had become an emperor, and his generals had been made princes, dukes and barons, all with great estates and hereditary titles. The Revolution had gone full circle.

Nevertheless, some 48,000 men became part of the Legion. Though only 1,200 of them were civilians, all were stipulated as being equals by Napoleon. ❖

NOTE:
1. Emile Ludwig, *Napoleon* (George Allen, London, 1935), pp.192-3.

Napoleon's Spanish Ulcer   Napoleon Bonaparte

Napoleon's Spanish Ulcer

The War in the Iberian Peninsula

It is sadly ironic that the attempted French conquest of the Iberian Peninsula – the longest continuous conflict of the Napoleonic Wars – was supposed to have been achieved peacefully. It would be accomplished, Napoleon is said to have remarked, 'with a few cannon shots'[1]. The seeds of that conflict, which became known as the Peninsular War, were sown on 21 November 1806, five weeks after defeating the once-mighty army of Prussia, when Napoleon issued a decree from the captured Prussian capital, Berlin, in which he outlawed all trade and correspondence between Britain and the French-controlled areas of Europe.

Britain then, as now, relied upon international commerce to maintain the expansion of its manufacturing industries. The restriction upon its trade caused by Napoleon's 'Continental System' caused some discomfort throughout the United Kingdom and export figures fell. Many countries in Europe, including alleged allies of France, nevertheless, disregarded the decrees and openly, or secretly, continued to trade with the 'Workshop of the World'. Napoleon was determined to stamp out this illicit trade and close off every continental port to British shipping.

MAIN PICTURE: *The bombardment of Copenhagen underway, this attack forming part of the United Kingdom's attempts to break or disrupt Napoleon's 'Continental System'. The original caption to this painting by H. Martens states that it illustrates the bombardment of the Danish port by the British forces between 2 and 5 September 1807, with soldiers and artillery pieces on a sand-spit, the burning city in the distance across an inlet. Note that Royal Navy warships can be seen firing in the right background.* (Anne S.K. Brown Military Collection, Brown University Library)

Napoleon Bonaparte Napoleon's Spanish Ulcer

After the Treaty of Tilsit, which was signed with Russia in July 1807, most of continental Europe was under Napoleon's sway, but Denmark, Sweden and Portugal still trafficked in British merchandise, the first as a neutral, the latter two as allies of King George. Aware that Napoleon intended to move into these three countries, Britain sent the Royal Navy to Copenhagen to demand that the Danish fleet be handed over to Great Britain for the duration of the war. Not unnaturally, the Crown Prince, Frederick, refused to give up his warships, whereupon the British fleet, command by Nelson, attacked the Danish warships whilst a British land force bombarded Copenhagen. Though the Danes capitulated, and their remaining undamaged ships were handed over to Nelson, this unprovoked attack, though considered necessary by the British Government, drove Denmark into the arms of Napoleon.

This left just Sweden and Portugal as the only avenues for British goods into Europe, and it was to Portugal that Napoleon next turned his attention. In an agreement with King Carlos of Spain, French troops marched across northern Spain and into Portugal, reaching Lisbon on 30 November 1807, just as the Portuguese royal family was sailing from the Portuguese capital, escorted by British warships, to the sanctuary of their colony of Brazil.

ABOVE: *A contemporary Danish painting, by the artist Christian William Eckersberg, of part of the bombardment of Copenhagen, which lasted from 16 August to 5 September 1807, as seen from the shore.*

Napoleon's Spanish Ulcer Napoleon Bonaparte

WILLIAM CONGREVE

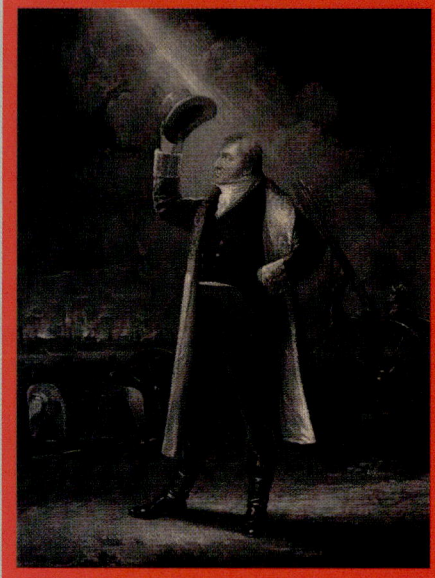

During the bombardment of Copenhagen, more than 14,000 missiles of various types, including metal balls, explosive and incendiary bombs from cannons and mortars, and about 300 Congreve rockets, were fired. The latter were designed and developed by Sir William Congreve in 1804, based on the design of the Mysorean rockets which were the first iron-cased rockets successfully deployed for military use. Due to the civilian evacuation of Copenhagen, the normal firefighting arrangements were ineffective and, consequently, over a thousand buildings were burned. The main user of Congreve rockets during the Napoleonic Wars was the Royal Navy, and men from the Royal Marine Artillery became experts in their use. This image depicts Congreve directing the fire of the rockets during the bombardment of Copenhagen. *(Anne S.K. Brown Military Collection, Brown University Library)*

Under the pretext of sending reinforcements to General Junot in Lisbon, more French troops entered Spain. But instead of marching across the border into Portugal, they continued southwards to Madrid. The imbecilic Carlos and his inept family were rounded up by Marshal Murat and despatched to France, with Napoleon's brother Joseph being made King of Spain.

Napoleon had assumed that the Spaniards would be happy to have an enlightened Bonaparte as their head of state instead of the corrupt and incapable Bourbons, but he was completely and disastrously wrong. First in Madrid, and then across the country, the Spanish people, men and women, rose up in revolt. King Joseph had scarcely settled into the Royal Palace before he was fleeing from the Spanish capital, not stopping until he was north of the River Ebro. There the French forces reformed in readiness to return to the offensive.

The Convention of Cintra

Though inveterate enemies since the days of Drake and the Spanish Armada, it was to Britain that the Spaniards turned for help in expelling the French from their country. Britain saw in the Spaniards an unlikely, though welcome, ally in its war against France and was quick to send arms and money to help fight the invading armies. A small force was quickly despatched to northern Spain under Sir Arthur Wellesley. The Spaniards, whilst quite happy to receive British gold and arms, were unwilling to have a British army marching across its land, and so it was to Portugal that Wellesley's men were directed. The British troops landed in Portugal on 1 August 1808, and, brushing aside the delaying forces sent by Junot, marched upon Lisbon.

Wellesley, at the time the most junior lieutenant general in the British Army, was succeeded by more senior generals, but by the time they had arrived, he had defeated Junot. However, before the British could take advantage of Wellesley's victory at the Battle of Vimeiro, Junot proposed an armistice. This was accepted by Lieutenant General Sir Hugh Dalrymple and subsequently converted into the Convention of Cintra.

RIGHT: *Portuguese and British troops fighting the French at Vimeiro, near Lisbon, on 21 August 1808. During the battle, the British under General Arthur Wellesley defeated the French under Major-General Jean-Andoche Junot, putting to an end the first French invasion of Portugal.*

BELOW: *The departure of the Prince Regent of Portugal, John VI of Portugal, and the royal family to Brazil in 1807.*

NAPOLEON BONAPARTE — NAPOLEON'S SPANISH ULCER

The Battle of Talavera, as depicted by Henri Leveque. (Anne S.K. Brown Military Collection, Brown University Library)

Under the terms of the Convention the French were allowed to retain their weapons and much of the plunder they had looted from the Portuguese. They were also to be repatriated to France in British ships and, upon their return, they were free to take up arms once again. When these details became known in London, Dalrymple was recalled to face a board of inquiry, with command of the British troops in Portugal devolving upon Sir John Moore, Wellesley having also returned to the UK.

Having at last accepted that they could not fight the French alone, the provisional Spanish government, the Supreme Junta, asked for Moore's force to coordinate with the Spanish armies in expelling the invaders. However, it would be Napoleon in person that Moore and the Spaniards would have to deal. This was because the Emperor's expectation of the easy subjugation of the Iberian Peninsula having foundered, he realised that he would have to intervene in person and 'get the machine working again'.

Transferring more than 100,000 of his most experienced troops from their garrisons in Germany and Italy, Napoleon crossed the Pyrenees and, brushing aside all opposition, reached Madrid on 1 December, reinstating his brother Joseph on the Spanish throne once again.

Moore, meanwhile, had advanced into northern Spain in a bid to sever Napoleon's lines of communication. When Napoleon became aware of this he turned his troops round and drove them on as fast as he could in a bid to encircle the British army. Moore, though, managed to escape to the port of Corunna, having to fight a delaying action before his troops could embark on the British ships, Moore being mortally wounded in the battle.

Sir Arthur Wellesley

Believing that with the recapture of Madrid and the expulsion of Moore's army he had crushed the Spanish rebellion, Napoleon returned to Paris, never to return to the Iberian Peninsula. But the proud Spaniards refused to accept a Bonaparte on the Spanish throne and a savage guerrilla war broke out. Attacks were made on isolated French outposts, couriers were ambushed and sentries were found with their throats cut. Atrocities were committed on both sides as the war took on a brutal character.

Despite Moore's army having been driven out of the Peninsula, the continuing unrest in Spain encouraged the British Government to persist with efforts to help the Spaniards. Sir Arthur Wellesley was sent back to Lisbon, which was still in British hands, and the army there reinforced.

The French, under Marshal Soult, had once again entered Portugal and Wellesley marched to meet them, defeating Soult at Oporto on 12 May 1809. Having liberated Portugal, Wellesley then attempted to operate in Spain in conjunction with the Spanish army of General Cuesta. The Spanish general proved a difficult ally and the operation ended when Wellesley had to fight a defensive battle against Joseph Bonaparte's forces at Talavera on 27–28 July 1809. Though the French were driven off, other enemy corps were marching hard to cut off the British line of retreat to Lisbon.

It was a close-run thing, but Wellesley managed to escape across the border back into Portugal, vowing, 'not to have anything to do with Spanish warfare on any grounds whatsoever, in the existing state of things'[2].

The ruins of part of Copenhagen after the British departure. On 5 September, the Danes sued for peace, and the capitulation was signed on 7 September. As part of this, Denmark agreed to surrender its navy and its naval stores. In return, the British undertook to leave Copenhagen within six weeks – which it did on 21 October 1807.

Napoleon's Spanish Ulcer — Napoleon Bonaparte

Wellesley, who was made Viscount Wellington for his victory at Talavera, knew that his army posed a threat to the French hold on Spain and that Napoleon would be certain to send a powerful force to drive the British out of Iberia once and for all. In the summer of 1810, that is exactly what Napoleon did.

The Lines of Torres Vedras

In many of the territories Napoleon had conquered the people of those lands saw the French troops as liberators, particularly in the regions of Italy which had long been under Austrian control, who brought with them enlightenment and an end to the old despotic rule. In other countries, the war was seen as a duel between kings and emperors and it mattered little to the peasantry who governed them. This began to change, firstly to some degree in Prussia because of the draconian penalties imposed upon the Germans, but then especially in Spain, and later in Russia.

Napoleon could not understand why the Spaniards did not want a liberal French-led regime. 'I expected their [the Spaniards] blessing,' he later said, 'but I was disappointed … they thought only of the insult'. He ascribed this to the interference of the British, or as he put it, 'the machinations of the English'[3]. If the British could be forced out of the Peninsula, he believed, the Spanish armies would be easily defeated and the country would settle down under its new, moderate but reforming, government. So, Napoleon placed a force, nominally some 130,000 strong, though in practice less than 100,000, under his most determined general, Marshal André Masséna, and ordered it to invade Portugal and drive the British into the sea.

But Wellington was well-prepared. He knew that his small British contingent of less than 30,000 men, with a further 20,000 or so untried Portuguese troops, could not contend with the experienced French soldiers in open battle. But after riding around the hills to the north of Lisbon he had seen that with skilful engineering, they could be turned into an almost impenetrable barrier behind which his army could hold back the French.

From November 1809, Wellington's Chief Engineer, Richard Fletcher, had been erecting a series of mutually-supporting forts, ravelins, redoubts and ditches across the Lisbon peninsula, work which had taken place under conditions of the utmost secrecy. Tens of thousands of men were employed on what became known as the Lines of Torres Vedras, which included blocking valleys and cutting the faces of the hillsides to make their slopes perpendicular. These lines were completed just in time, as Masséna captured the border fortresses of Ciudad Rodrigo and Almeida and advanced into north-central Portugal.

A view of the Battle of Buçaco, showing Reynier's II Corps attacking San Antonio de Cantaro, on 27 September 1810. (Anne S.K. Brown Military Collection, Brown University Library)

ABOVE: *An original watercolour by the renowned military artist Lady E. Butler, depicting Wellington and staff mounted and at the salute, on the left, watching soldiers carrying wounded and dead at the Battle of Talavera, July 1809. (Anne S.K. Brown Military Collection, Brown University Library)*

BELOW: *British troops, and other elements of the Allied army, fording the River Mondego on 21 September 1810 in the lead-up to the Battle of Buçaco six days later. (Anne S.K. Brown Military Collection, Brown University Library)*

General Craufurd's headquarters at Buçaco – Craufurd commanded the Light Division during the battle. These small circular windmills were found throughout Portugal and many were incorporated into the Lines of Torres Vedras as secondary strongpoints or as observation posts.
(John Grehan Collection)

SIEGE OF CADIZ

When Napoleon's forces reached southern Spain, the Spanish government retreated into the fortress-port of Cadiz. In a bid to try and bombard Cadiz, Napoleon's craftsmen cast this enormous mortar, the shells of which were able to reach into the very heart of the city. This mortar can be seen today in Horse Guards Parade, London. Its inscription reads: 'To Commemorate the raising of the siege of Cadiz, in consequence of the Glorious Victory, gained by the Duke of Wellington over the French near Salamanca … This Mortar, cast for the destruction of that great port, with powers surpassing all others, and abandoned by the Besiegers on their Retreat, was presented as a token of respect and gratitude by the Spanish Nation to His Royal Highness the Prince Regent.'
(John Grehan Collection)

As the French continued towards Lisbon, the Portuguese people left their homes as they had been instructed, driving their livestock before them, after destroying their crops. The French found themselves marching through a virtual desert.

After turning on Masséna, and inflicting a damaging defeat on the French army at Buçaco, Wellington withdrew into the Lines. On 11 October 1810, the French reached the Lines. It was as far as they got.

After probing attacks upon parts of the Line, it was clear that the fortifications, backed by the Anglo-Portuguese army, were too strong to be assaulted. Though Masséna hung on until March 1811, eventually hunger and dwindling resources induced him to abandon the operation and he marched his depleted army back to Spain.

A War of Logistics

Spain, it was said, was a country where small armies were defeated and large armies starved. This meant that the French, though generally more than 250,000 strong, could only concentrate their forces into large armies for relatively short periods of time before they were compelled to disperse to find food. Wellington was acutely aware of this and after seizing the Spanish border fortresses of Ciudad Rodrigo in the north and Badajoz in the south, he knew that he could strike at the French across the border from the security of his Portuguese base at will and that it would take many days, or even weeks, for the French commanders in Spain to be able to gather together sufficient strength the face the British. To be able to raise a force strong enough to meet Wellington, the French had to strip their garrisons, which enabled the Spanish armies and guerrillas to rise up and attack the weakened outposts, taking back some of the places won at great cost by the French. Wellington was also able to defeat the various French armies, achieving notable victories at Fuentes de Oñoro, Salamanca and Vitoria. Added to this, the Spanish armies, though invariably beaten, would reform and fight again, and it was said that in large parts of Spain French authority extended no further than the range of their muskets.

The result was that the Peninsula was never fully subdued and was a constant drain on Napoleon's resources, with an almost continual reinforcement of fresh troops being required to replace the losses through battle and illness. Almost 300,000 French and their allies had been killed or wounded in the Peninsula by the time Napoleon abdicated in 1814.

The Peninsular War was the longest continuous conflict during the Napoleonic era, lasting for just two weeks less than six years. Napoleon called it his 'Spanish ulcer' and it slowly bled his armies dry. Its effects were felt far beyond the Pyrenees, with Wellington's great victories showing the rest of Europe that Napoleon's armies were not invincible, giving the Emperor's enemies hope and the determination to fight on. ❖

Masséna's retreat from Portugal begins. (Anne S.K. Brown Military Collection, Brown University Library)

NOTES:
1. Quoted in John Grehan, *The Battle of Barossa, Forgotten Battle of the Peninsular War* (Pen & Sword, Barnsley, 2012), p.vii.
2. Quoted in John Grehan, *The Lines of Torres Vedras, Wellington's Cornerstone in the Peninsular War 1809-12* (Frontline, Barnsley, 2015), p.7.
3. Both of these quotes are reproduced in Ian Fletcher [Ed.], *The Peninsular War, Aspects of the Struggle for the Iberian Peninsula* (Spellmount, Staplehurst, 1998), p.33.

NAPOLEON'S EMPIRE   NAPOLEON BONAPARTE

NAPOLEON'S

Napoleon's influence extended throughout the length and breadth of Europe. It would prove short-lived, however, and his meteoric rise would be matched only by its precipitous fall.

It is usually said that Napoleon reached the height of his power in 1807, after his alliance with Tsar Alexander of Russia, but at that time his empire was still expanding, reaching its maximum extent in 1812 – just before its dramatic collapse.

The Empire was composed of three elements. These comprised the land governed and administered by France, the *Pays Réunis*; the countries conquered by Napoleon, the *Pays Conquis*; and the *Pays Alliés*.

The *Pays Réunis* was composed of the departments of France plus the area of Greater France which had been pushed out to what was regarded as its natural frontiers i.e. the Rhine, the Alps and the Pyrenees. This territory encompassed Belgium and Holland, parts of Germany and the Italian coast all the way down to Rome, including Piedmont, Parma, the Papal States, Tuscany, the Illyrian Provinces. Including France, this embraced forty-four million people.

The countries of the *Pays Conquis*, though supposedly independent, were ruled by Napoleon's nominees, usually his relatives. These included the Confederation of the Rhine, Spain, Naples, the Duchy of Warsaw and other parts of Italy.

The *Pays Alliés* were those states allied to France, which, in 1811 were Prussia, Bavaria, Austria and Russia. These formed the Grand Empire, which, at its peak, had 80 million people within its borders.

EMPIRE

NAPOLEON BONAPARTE | NAPOLEON'S EMPIRE

BLOOD IN THE SNOW · NAPOLEON BONAPARTE

BLOOD IN THE SNOW

Napoleon's Invasion of Russia, 1812

ABOVE: *A portrait of General Pyotr Bagration which can be seen in The Hermitage. A few days before Napoleon's invasion on 24 June, he suggested to Alexander I a pre-emptive strike into the Duchy of Warsaw.*

England, and, after 1707, Britain, had fought against France in every century from the 1200s, often with only brief periods of uneasy peace between the two nations. Just six years before Napoleon had been born, the Seven Years' War had ended in defeat for France, and he was just nine years old when the two countries were again fighting in the Anglo-French War of 1778-1783. Ten years later saw the start of the French Revolutionary War. He had grown up, boy and man, to view Britain as France's inveterate enemy and if France was to have the peace and stability which Napoleon sought, Britain would have to be defeated, once and for all.

With, in Napoleon's eyes, Britain being 'a nation of shopkeepers', he knew that the most effective way of bringing Britain down was by engaging in economic warfare. The result, as we have already read, was his introduction of the Continental System, announced through the Berlin Decree, on 21 November 1806. This, though an understandable tactic, proved to be

MAIN PICTURE: *Hectic and chaotic scenes such as this were typical of the French crossing of the River Berezina, near Borisov in Belarus, in November 1812. Despite the fact many of Napoleon's troops managed to cross the river, their losses were considerable, so much so that since the campaign the word 'Bérézina' has been used in French as a synonym for 'disaster'.*

a perfect example of the law of unintended consequences. For Britain responded in a similar fashion the following year with the Orders in Council which forbade French trade with the United Kingdom, its allies, or neutrals, and instructed the Royal Navy to blockade French and allied ports.

Hardship was felt on both sides of the Channel because of the enormous collapse in international trade. This was particularly felt by those countries allied to France which had long traditions of trading with Britain and had been forced into compliance with the Berlin Decree through the fear of French force of arms. But Czar Alexander, far to the north and a long way from France, had less to fear than most, and increasingly Russia slipped in its enforcement of the Continental System. There were other issues between France and Russia, both of which had expansionist ambitions, which led to growing anti-French sentiment in St Petersburg. This situation had to be resolved one way or another. It was Napoleon's way to use force to achieve his ends, and from the beginning of 1811, he started to plan the most ambitious campaign of his career – the invasion of the largest country in the world, Russia.

A depiction of Napoleon's forces crossing the River Niemen at the start of the Campaign of 1812.

The Grand Armée

Napoleon did not underestimate the size of the task he had set himself, and he assembled what was possibly the largest army seen in Europe to that date. In total, he amassed a staggering 675,000 troops, including reserves and those on supply and garrison duties. These troops were drawn not just from France but from every allied and satellite state, even including, if somewhat unwillingly, an Austrian corps and a contingent from Prussia. The Czar was only able to deploy little more than 200,000 men, with the forces facing Napoleon being divided into two wings under generals Pyotr Bagration and Michael Andreas Barclay de Tolly. ➤

Blood In The Snow   Napoleon Bonaparte

ABOVE: *General Nikolay Rayevski leading a detachment of the Russian Imperial Guard into combat at the Battle of Saltanovka, 23 July 1812. The engagement, an attempt to halt Napoleon's advance, resulted in a French victory, despite the determination of Rayevski's men who inflicted nearly twice as many casualties as they suffered. The battle prevented Bagration from joining forces with Barclay de Tolly.*

Napoleon's campaign plan, put in very simple terms, was to hold the Russian centre around Warsaw with part of the Grande Armée under his youngest brother Jérôme, which included the Austrian corps led by Prince Schwarzenberg, whilst the main body, of mostly French regiments under his personal command, swung round to the left to take the Russians in the flank. Whilst the plan was sound, the scale of the operation, both in terms of distance and manpower, was too great to be controlled in the days when the fastest medium of communication was by horse and often over poor roads and difficult terrain. Generals of the early nineteenth century relied to a great degree on being able to exert direct personal control of their armies, and in the vast regions of Poland and Russia it proved simply impossible for Napoleon to coordinate his forces to deliver the telling blow that would knock out the Russian army.

Nevertheless, the Grande Armée crossed the River Nieman on 24 June 1812. Napoleon expected to make contact with the Russian outposts at an early stage, but instead of defending their ground, the enemy was found to be withdrawing. Even at this juncture, the movement of large bodies of troops in perfect harmony was proving problematical, and Napoleon had to slow his advance to allow the corps under his stepson, Eugène de Beauharnais (Joséphine's son), to catch up. Napoleon had achieved many of his most notable victories through his speed of manoeuvre; now his armies were moving slower than those of his opponent.

It has been long debated whether or not Alexander intended from the outset to retreat and allow the French armies to march deep into the vastness of Russia or whether, as seems more likely, such a policy was forced upon him by Napoleon's movements and the sheer weight of his forces.

ABOVE: *A painting of Prince Michael Andreas Barclay de Tolly which, completed when he held the rank of Field Marshal, hangs in the Military Gallery of the Winter Palace in Saint Petersburg, Russia.*

BELOW: *A view of the fighting during the Battle of Smolensk on 17 August 1812. This was the first major battle of the French invasion of Russia. The battle, which lasted from 16 to 18 August, involved between 175,000 men of the Grande Armée under Napoleon and 130,000 Russians under Barclay de Tolly. To save his forces, de Tolly abandoned the city, destroying all ammunition stores and bridges, leaving a small force to hold out for two days to cover his retreat.*

NAPOLEON BONAPARTE BLOOD IN THE SNOW

ABOVE: *An aerial view of part of the battlefield at Borodino. The memorial that dominates the image stands on the site of the Raevsky Redoubt. A massive open-backed earthwork mounting nineteen 12-pounder cannon, the redoubt defended the centre of the Russian positions during the battle, and was the location of some of the bloodiest fighting.* (Mitrofanov Alexander/Shutterstock)

ABOVE: *A painting by Peter Heinrich Lambert von Hess of the Battle of Borodino, 7 September 1812. The battle was famously described by Count Leo Tolstoy, in his novel* War and Peace, *as 'a continuous slaughter which could be of no avail either to the French or the Russians'.*

Slipped The Net

Soon, the pace of Napoleon's advance slowed even further, as heavy rains turned the poor roads into quagmires, which made movement for the heavy supply wagons even more difficult – and it was still the height of summer. This meant that instead of Jérôme engaging General Bagration and pinning him down, whilst Napoleon manoeuvred round the Russian flank, the Russian commander was able to withdraw virtually unmolested. Napoleon was furious, telling his brother that he had robbed him, 'of the fruit of my manoeuvres and of the best opportunity ever presented in war'.

Having failed to trap the enemy and deliver the crushing blow that could have ended the campaign, Napoleon was in something of a quandary, especially as other elements of the Grande Armée were also far behind schedule. He therefore devised a second plan, turning

The effects of this policy, whether created by accident or design, very quickly began to be felt by the Grande Armée. Even before the end of June the advancing troops, though moving slow compared with Napoleon's usual operations, had outstripped the lumbering supply wagons and the men were becoming hungry, exacerbated by the actions of the Russians troops, as Carl von Clausewitz explained: 'It was the custom with the Russian rear-guard to burn every village as they abandoned it. The inhabitants were generally withdrawn beforehand; what they contained in forage and subsistence was rapidly used and nothing therefore remained but the wooden houses, which in this country are of little value … [this] extended itself widely to the towns, great as well as small.'[1]

Inevitably, this meant the French soldiers had to search far from the line of march to find sustenance, which further reduced the rate of advance.

ABOVE: *Part of the remaining earthworks that formed the Raevsky Redoubt at Borodino. Interestingly, a visitor to Borodino today can also see remnants of trenches dug during the seven-day battle fought on the same battlefield in 1941 between Soviet and German forces.* (Michkasova Elena/Shutterstock)

Blood In The Snow — Napoleon Bonaparte

THE SHEVARDINO REDOUBT

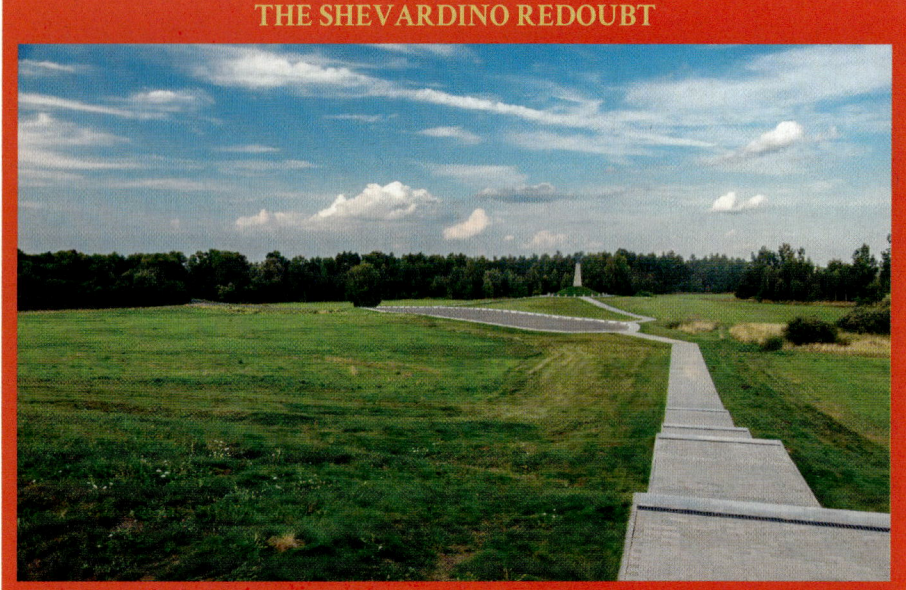

The site of the Shevardino Redoubt on the Borodino battlefield. The initial Russian position at Borodino, which stretched south of a new post road to Smolensk (Napoleon's expected route of advance), was anchored on its left by a pentagonal earthwork redoubt erected on a mound near the village of Shevardino. The Redoubt was of particular importance in the lead-up to the battle. The monument that can be seen in the background is the so-called 'French Memorial'. This was unveiled in 1913 with the consent of the Russian government, having been paid for and erected by the French, in memory of those members of the Grande Armée who fell at Borodino. It stands on the spot where Napoleon established a command post during the battle on 7 September 1812. *(Masterovoy/Shutterstock)*

It was a terrible, and uncharacteristic, mistake. When he drew up his army in full battle order on the 28th to attack Vitebsk (now a city in Belarus), he found no enemy to fight.

The Flames of Smolensk

There was no longer any need for Napoleon to drive his men relentlessly on. The Russians had a day's march on the French, and with every step were shortening their supply lines, whilst those of the Grande Armée were lengthening. Napoleon now knew that he faced a long, gruelling campaign, and he needed to allow his tired and hungry troops to recover before continuing. Already the corpses of hundreds of men and thousands of horses marked the route of the French advance, and Cossacks had begun to harass the marching columns with demoralising hit and run tactics. These daring horsemen would strike at stragglers or create delays whilst the French infantry stopped to receive them, only for the Cossacks to merrily ride off having caused chaos but without any risk of danger to themselves.

For eight days Napoleon rested his troops. The efforts to bring the Russians to battle had seen his huge army become extended over a front of some 500 miles. Napoleon had little

his attention to the other wing of the Russian army under Barclay. Again, one part of his force would hold the Russian front whilst another moved north to cut Barclay's communications with St Petersburg, the Russian capital.

Barclay, however, had no intention of getting caught, aiming to join with Bagration. Napoleon managed to place his main body between the two Russian armies and with Murat's cavalry in contact with its Russian counterparts it looked as if, finally, Napoleon had compelled one wing of the Russian army to fight. Believing that crucial battle was now at hand, Napoleon resisted the urge to attack at once and waited for a day – 27 July 1812 – for reinforcements to join him.

RIGHT: *As the men of the Grande Armée found out to their cost, the Cossacks, predominantly horsemen from the Russian steppes, were ideally suited to reconnaissance, scouting and harassing the enemy's flanks and supply lines.*

BELOW: *Napoleon on the battlefield at Borodino.* (Oleg Golovnev/Shutterstock)

effective control of the outlying elements of his force, and, worse, no plan other than to march into Russia.

The halt at Vitebsk allowed de Tolly and Bagration to join up. Together their combined force amounted to around 125,000 men and, under pressure from Alexander and the great and the good of St Petersburg and Moscow, they made a stand at the fortress city of Smolensk. Napoleon, it appeared, would at last have the battle he sought.

Believing that the Russians would fight outside Smolensk to save the historic city from destruction, on 17 August, French troops stormed the suburbs. But Barclay refused to be drawn from behind the safety of the city walls. So Napoleon brought up 200 guns and began to bombard Smolensk. Soon the city was on fire, and the walls badly damaged, but the attackers were without ladders or any scaling equipment and, under fire from the defenders, were unable to break into Smolensk. The city burned throughout

NAPOLEON BONAPARTE ✦ BLOOD IN THE SNOW

ABOVE: *General Kutuzov, on the far left, is depicted here during a military council he held with his senior officers prior to taking the decision to surrender, and abandon, Moscow to Napoleon – some of those present had objected to this action being taken. This meeting is described as having taken place in the home of a peasant by the name of A.S. Frolov in the village of Fili. It was to there that the Russian army had retreated after the Battle of Borodino, setting up camp near the village on 12 September. Today Fili is part of the western suburbs of Moscow.*

the night. The next morning Polish troops under Napoleon managed to break through into the city, but Barclay had moved out during the night.

Losses during the battle were around even, though figures vary from between 4,000 to 14,000 on both sides – and the Russians had escaped once again. What also seemed alarming was that the Russians did not bother to protect one of the most venerated cities in their country by going out into the open to meet the invaders. They would rather let their homes burn than risk defeat at the hands of the French. Just how determined the Russians were would become even more apparent in the weeks to come.

The Deadliest Day

Napoleon halted for six days whilst he considered his options. He could have set himself down on Russian soil and waited for Alexander to rise to the challenge, but he chose instead to march on – towards Moscow.

It was far from unknown that a Russian czar would be quietly disposed of if seen as a liability, as indeed had been Alexander's father, Paul I. With Napoleon marching ever deeper into Russia, and with Moscow evidently his next objective, Alexander knew he had to take decisive action. Barclay de Tolly was therefore removed from his post of overall commander of the Russian forces, and in his place stepped the redoubtable sixty-seven-year-old Prince Mikhail Illarionovich Golenishchev-Kutuzov.

Kutuzov knew that Barclay's tactics had been the correct ones to adopt, as the further the French marched the greater their wastage in both men and materiel. But he also knew he had to fight a battle to ease the fears of the Russian people and to raise the morale of the army which had deteriorated at having to continually retreat.

Kutuzov, though, needed time to establish a good defensive position, so he employed a strong rearguard to impede the advance of the French, whilst he found suitable ground for the great clash of arms that could no longer be avoided. That clash occurred less than eighty miles from Moscow.

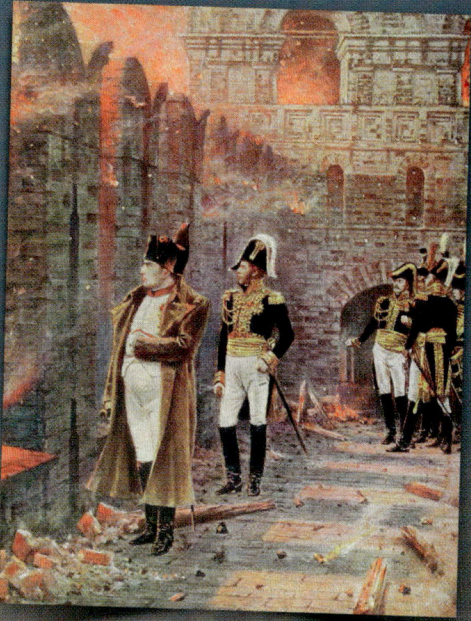

ABOVE: *Napoleon watches Moscow burn from the walls of the Kremlin itself.*

BELOW: *In this painting by the artist Adam Albrecht, Napoleon, depicted as he often is on horseback, watches the burning of Moscow, the fire having first broken out on 14 September 1812. The burning of Moscow is reported to have been visible up to 215 kilometres away.*

71

Blood In The Snow   Napoleon Bonaparte

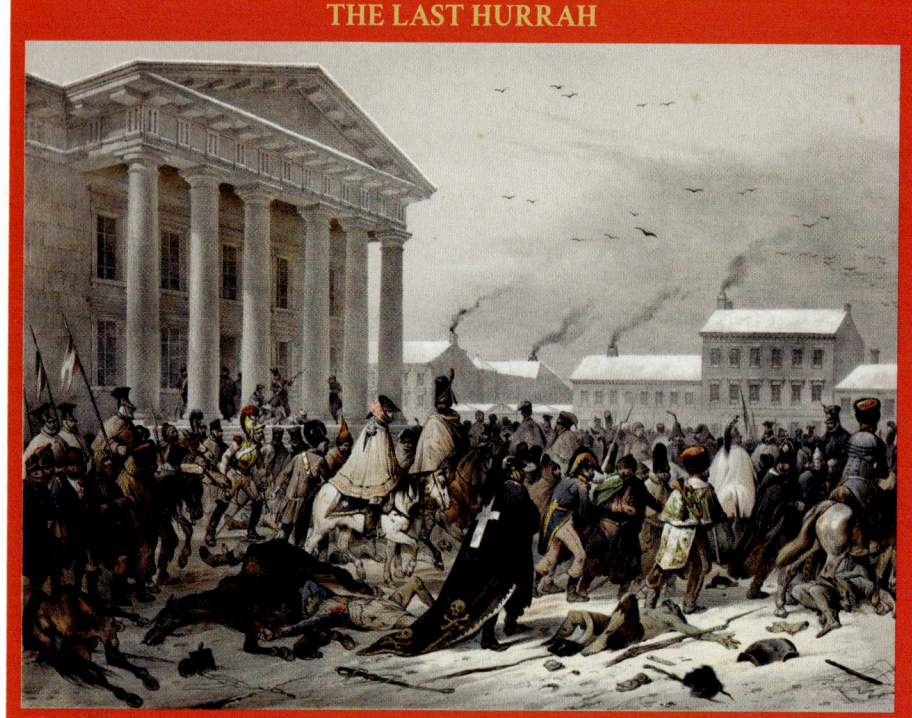

THE LAST HURRAH

They had marched with the Emperor Napoleon as part of the greatest assembly of warriors the world had seen, but they were never to return home. The remains of some 3,000 of Napoleon's soldiers were uncovered from a mass grave during construction work in Vilnius, the capital of Lithuania. These once-proud soldiers are now just bones, yet some of them have remnants of clothing attached to their skeletal remains, which have shown that men from more than forty regiments were buried there. The remains were packed into the grave at a ratio of around seven bodies for every square metre of ground. The majority were male with only around twenty being female, and most were in their twenties.

As the Grande Armée retreated from Moscow, it crossed Belarus and marched on to Vilnius – the image seen here depicts French troops in the city's main square. By this stage of the retreat the men were in poor condition, and examinations of the remains have shown just how badly the men were suffering. Chemical analysis of the bones has revealed that many had contracted typhus and the presence of high levels of nitrogen suggest that they were starving and were suffering from hypothermia due to the severe cold. What the studies have also revealed is where they probably came from. Of the eight males and one female whose bones were subjected to oxygen isotope analysis, it was found that most were from central and western Europe, with three individuals possibly coming from the Iberian Peninsula and one who may have participated in an African campaign before the Russian one. Additionally, the one woman who was tested may have hailed from southern France.

We know that some Portuguese troops joined the Grande Armée and that there were Mamluks with Napoleon's Imperial Guard, so surprising these facts may at first seem, they were entirely consistent with what we know about the composition of the forces that invaded Russia in 1812 – and, of course, it was in southern France that the spirit of the Revolution found its voice, which continues today in the *Marseillaise*.

On 7 September 1812, Napoleon attacked the Russian line near the village of Borodino. By this time, Napoleon's huge army had shrunk to such an extent that the battle was fought against almost even numbers and resulted in a hard-fought draw. The Russian defence was formed around a number of strong fieldworks which were assaulted by the French at considerable cost. By mid-afternoon, the Russians appeared to be on the point of collapse, and Napoleon was urged to commit the Imperial Guard to finish off the enemy. Napoleon refused. The Emperor was guilty of many errors of judgement during the Russian campaign, but his desire to keep his Guard intact rather than use them to finish off the Russians at Borodino was probably his most egregious mistake.

Kutuzov was able to withdraw with his forces largely intact, though much reduced in numbers, having lost around 40,000 men. The French army, likewise, suffered more than 30,000 casualties. Such losses on both sides has meant that 7 September has entered the history books as the deadliest single day of the entire Napoleonic Wars.

The Burning of Moscow

Kutuzov retreated, leaving the road to Moscow open. A week after Borodino, on 14 September, Napoleon entered Moscow – and found it empty. All but a few thousand of the city's 275,000-strong population had simply packed up and left. Amongst those who remained were a few men given the task of denying Moscow to the invaders, by burning it to the ground.

Napoleon, who had retired to a house on the outskirts of the city for the night, was woken in the early hours of the 15th with the news that Russians had been seen setting fire to buildings in the city. The Emperor went to the Kremlin to see for himself, and was nearly caught up in the blaze.

When the flames died down three days later more than two-thirds of Russia's largest city had been burnt to the ground. With Kutuzov prepared to retreat even deeper into the barren Russian wastes, and with no shelter and precious little food for his troops, Napoleon had no choice but to abandon his great enterprise before the onset of the feared Russia winter.

The Comte de Ségur, one of Napoleon's closest aides, put into words why Napoleon failed to defeat the Russians: 'The nobles retreated into the interior with the serfs, as if at the approach of a deadly plague, sacrificing riches, homes, everything that might detain them or be of any use to us. They put hunger, fire, and the desert between themselves and us; for it was as much in fear of their serfs as of Napoleon that this high resolution was carried out. It was no longer a war of kings that we were fighting, but a class war, a party war, a religious war, a national war – all sorts of war rolled into one.'[2]

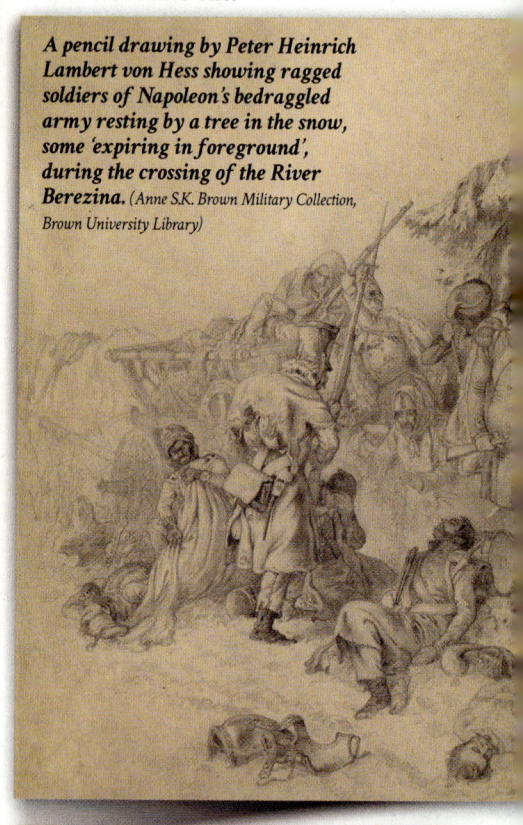

A pencil drawing by Peter Heinrich Lambert von Hess showing ragged soldiers of Napoleon's bedraggled army resting by a tree in the snow, some 'expiring in foreground', during the crossing of the River Berezina. (Anne S.K. Brown Military Collection, Brown University Library)

ABOVE: *An unusual relic from the Grande Armée's retreat – a captured field kitchen. It is on display in the Museum of the Patriotic War of 1812 in Moscow. (Aleks49/Shutterstock)*

NAPOLEON BONAPARTE — BLOOD IN THE SNOW

The Retreat

All that was left for Napoleon to do was to try and get back to France with as much of his army intact as possible, as the first snows of winter began to fall. He had to travel back along the same ravaged route as he had advanced, and it was now the Russians' turn to attack, harassing the line of march at every opportunity.

The greatest tragedy for the Grande Armée during the retreat occurred between 26 and 29 November when it reached the River Berezina where the Russian commander Admiral Pavel Chichagov, with a force of 34,000 soldiers, was waiting, having destroyed the bridge at Borisov on the line of the French retreat. Other Russian forces, including the 40,000-strong main army under Kutuzov, were bearing down on Borisov.

If Napoleon could not force the passage of the river his army would be annihilated. In an unfortunate twist of fate, the 100-yard-wide Berezina, which would normally have been frozen over at that time of year, thereby permitting the Grande Armée an easy crossing, was in full flood. Napoleon's only hope lay in his engineers being able to raise a temporary bridge. To do this, one corps under Marshal Oudinot drew the Russians away and two rough bridges were thrown across the Berezina. Of course, Chichagov was not deceived for long and attacked, by which time the bulk of Napoleon's army was safely across; but at least 15,000 men had been lost.

Wearily, the Grande Armée marched on, but Napoleon's once-mighty army, the greatest to march to war, no longer bore even the semblance of a military force. Franz Joseph Hausemann, serving with General Wrede's detached Bavarian Corps, saw the main body of Napoleon's army on 6 December: 'What a sight! For many hours, Wrede's command had to march along next to this whirling human river, which was wrapped in every sort of costume and dress, and which seemed to be composed of every race. No one can depict the astonishment, no one the impression, which the sight of so many thousand figures, lost to all discipline and order, unarmed, mostly wrapped in rags, given over to the most frightful misery, made upon the morale of each and every common soldier … instead of a battle-ready, confident army, still powerful despite its great misfortunes … only a defenceless mass of half-frozen, half-starved creatures staggering by in a wild jumble.'[3]

One of Napoleon's artillery commanders, Colonel Jean Noël, painted a similar scene in his memoirs: 'The appearance of this disorderly mob was truly pitiful. It is impossible to imagine a more tragic picture … It was a rabble, a mass of haggard men, slovenly, and in rags, who stumbled forward lurching into each other … All ranks were muddled together, officers and troops, cavalry and infantry, French, Italians and Germans, without their weapons, clad in tattered finery, cloaks, sacks, the skins of newly killed animals, and with footwear made from old clothes and hats.' This human tragedy was, as Noël correctly diagnosed, 'the mad ambition of a single man'.[4]

By the time that Noël and Hausemann witnessed the state of the French army, Napoleon had already left his men, riding on as quickly as he could with a small escort of Neapolitan cavalry. There was little point in him trudging along with his men; he had to return to Paris as soon as he could to raise a new army, for he knew that all his enemies would see the best opportunity they would ever have of defeating him. 'I can only maintain my grip of Europe from the Tuileries,' Napoleon declared. There were more battles ahead before the Emperor of the French would relinquish his throne. ❖

ABOVE: *French engineers battle to construct the temporary bridges across the River Berezina.*
(Morphart Creation/Shutterstock)

James Atkinson's painting of Napoleon being jeered at by ragged and dishevelled members of his Grande Armée during the retreat in 1812.
(Anne S.K. Brown Military Collection, Brown University Library)

NOTES:

1. Carl con Clausewitz, *The Campaign in Russia, A Prussian Officer's Account from Russian Headquarters* (Frontline, Barnsley, 2015), pp.179-80.
2. Quoted in J. Christopher Herold, *The Age of Napoleon* (Penguin, London, 1963), p.318.
3. John H. Gill (Ed.), *A Soldier for Napoleon: The Campaigns of Lieutenant Franz Joseph Hausmann, 7th Bavarian Infantry* (Frontline, Barnsley, 2016), p.109.
4. Colonel Jean-Nicolas-Auguste Noël, edited and translated by R. Brindle, *With Napoleon's Guns, The Military Memoirs of an Officer of the First Empire* (Frontline, Barnsley, 2016), p.144.

SUBSCRIBE

FlyPast is internationally regarded as the magazine for aviation history and heritage.

shop.keypublishing.com/fpsubs

FREE GIFT WORTH £33.95!

Britain at War is dedicated to exploring every aspect of the involvement of Britain and her Commonwealth in conflicts from the turn of the 20th century through to the present day.

shop.keypublishing.com/bawsubs

FREE GIFT WORTH £35.95!

ORDER DIRECT FROM OUR SHOP...
shop.keypublish

OR CALL **+44 (0)1780 480404**

(Lines open 9.00-5.30, Monday-Friday GMT)

Key Publishing

TODAY

SAVE UP TO £30 WHEN YOU SUBSCRIBE!

Aeroplane is still providing the best aviation coverage around. With focus on iconic military aircraft from the 1930s to the 1960s.

shop.keypublishing.com/amsubs

FREE GIFT WORTH £28.94!

Classic Military Vehicle is the best-selling publication in the UK dedicated to the coverage of all historic military vehicles.

shop.keypublishing.com/cmvsubs

FREE GIFT WORTH £26.94!

ing.com

BATTLE OF THE NATIONS NAPOLEON BONAPARTE

BATTLE OF THE

The invasion of Russia had destroyed Napoleon's Grand Armée and presented his enemies with a chance to finally bring him down. The opposing sides met at the Saxon city of Leipzig, in what was to be the largest battle in Europe before the First World War.

NAPOLEON BONAPARTE | BATTLE OF THE NATIONS

Nations

MAIN PICTURE: *A hand-coloured engraving depicting the Battle of Bautzen on 20–21 May 1813. The town itself can be seen in the background. Although a success for the French, Bautzen was not the decisive, strategic victory Napoleon desperately sought.* (Anne S.K. Brown Military Collection, Brown University Library)

No-one knows for certain how many men died during Napoleon's ill-fated Russian campaign but only around 100,000 survived, of whom just 35,000 were French soldiers. Allowing for desertions early on in the campaign before the Grand Armée reached hostile territory, something around 400,000 men died of disease and starvation or were killed by enemy action, the rest of that magnificent force being taken prisoner, including forty-eight generals.[1] The Russians, it is believed, suffered little more than half that number of casualties.

With the Russians continuing to advance into central Europe, Napoleon had to raise another army, which he achieved by arming pensioners, rounding up 'draft-dodgers' from earlier conscriptions and bringing forward the class of 1814 a year early. Astonishingly, by the summer of 1813, he had managed to cobble together a field army 400,000 strong. But what could not be so easily replaced were the 200,000 trained horses that had been lost or the 1,050 cannon that had been left behind in Russia. When Napoleon had to fight again, he would do so with inadequate numbers of cavalry and artillery and with few experienced soldiers. Nor could he even draw from his army in Spain as Wellington was proving too difficult an opponent for his marshals to contend with. ➤

Battle Of The Nations — Napoleon Bonaparte

ABOVE: *General Blücher, commander of the Prusso-Russian army that was defeated at Bautzen, is pictured here in the hill-top Saxon town prior to his withdrawal.*

Napoleon's defeat in Russia led to the formation of yet another coalition, the sixth, against France, in which Russia was joined by Britain, Sweden and Prussia amongst the more powerful nations. If Napoleon could field an impressive army, it was small compared with the numbers which the Allies could count, with some 800,000 assembling in the new front line in Germany along with a strategic reserve of another 350,000 men.

But before these forces could be properly organised and a plan of campaign formulated, Napoleon struck with his former speed and brilliance.

Lützen and Bautzen

At the end of April, Napoleon led an army of some 170,000 men directly towards the Coalition forces in a bid to destroy them individually before they could become unified. He expected to encounter the first Coalition troops at Dresden, but, because of the failings of his inexperienced cavalry, he was surprised to learn that a combined Prussian and Russian force was close by at Lützen near Leipzig. Quickly realising that he had been presented with an unexpected gift, Napoleon left one corps under Marshal Ney to lure the Allies towards where the rest of his army was waiting. The Prussian General Blücher, in command of the Allied force, took the bait and attacked Ney, who withdrew, drawing the enemy towards the positions of a powerful battery of guns. Following this storm of shot and shell, Napoleon launched an assault, led by the Imperial Guard, upon the flank of the advancing Allies. By nightfall the Allies were in headlong retreat, but the Battle of Lützen cost Napoleon dear, with casualties of approximately 20,000 - men that he could ill afford to lose.

Blücher and the Russian general Wittgenstein retreated to Bautzen on the River Spree, where they were ordered to make a stand by their respective monarchs. Pursuing the Allies, Napoleon attacked them at Bautzen and won yet another victory. So much so, that on 2 June the Allies asked for an armistice, to which the Emperor agreed. Both sides knew that this was not the end of the fighting, and when hostilities resumed on 2 August, Austria had joined the Coalition – Napoleon's own father-in-law had turned against him.

Dresden

Napoleon sought, as always, to bring his enemies to battle in one great encounter. But the Allies had finally learnt how to defeat the Emperor. The Russian campaign had shown how he could be beaten – by withdrawing the main body of their forces whilst subsidiary elements struck at the French until they were weakened to such a degree the Allies

ABOVE: *Russian Cossacks in Bautzen during the fighting in the area in 1813. In one of the last battles on the Eastern Front during the Second World War, Russian troops again fought in the countryside surrounding Bautzen at the end of April 1945, though on this occasion they were fighting German forces.*

BELOW: *Austrian troops from the Army of Bohemia and French infantry clash during the Battle of Dresden, 26 August 1813.* (Anne S.K. Brown Military Collection, Brown University Library)

NAPOLEON BONAPARTE — BATTLE OF THE NATIONS

ABOVE: *A portrait of Marshal Étienne Jacques Joseph Alexandre MacDonald, whose actions cost Napoleon's forces some 15,000 men and 100 cannon. Though MacDonald was born in Sedan, France, his father, Neil MacEachen, later MacDonald, came from a Jacobite family which had its origins on South Uist in the Outer Hebrides. He was a close relative of Flora MacDonald, who played a key role in the escape of Prince Charles Edward Stuart after the failure of the 1745 Rising.*

ABOVE: *An unusual relic of the Battle of Dresden is this 'Napoleon Stone' which can be seen in the Schloßplatz in Dresden. It marks the spot where Napoleon reviewed his troops before they marched out of the city to fight the Coalition forces. (Courtesy of Henry Mühlpfordt)*

ABOVE: *Napoleon rides into Dresden in 1813. (Morphart Creation/Shutterstock)*

could make a stand with every expectation of success. This was formulated into what was called the Trachenberg Plan[2].

This final, decisive, campaign of Napoleon's first reign as Emperor, began as the opposing sides expected, with the Allies retreating as Napoleon pushed deeper into Germany. Napoleon believed that his enemies were running scared but that he would soon catch and destroy them.

As Napoleon advanced, his various corps did, indeed, catch up with some of the Allied forces, most notably the Prussians under Blücher. On each occasion that they clashed, the French were left masters of the field, but each engagement cost Napoleon dear, in both men and, alarmingly, ammunition. Napoleon was hampered by his lack of efficient light cavalry – the eyes and ears of the army – and had little real idea of the movements of his enemies or of their strength.

It was this lack of knowledge which caused Napoleon to suddenly change his plans when Marshal Saint-Cyr announced that he was facing the entire Austrian Army of Bohemia, 200,000 strong, at Dresden. Napoleon marched with the Imperial Guard to join Saint-Cyr and though outnumbered three to two, over the course of 26-27 August 1813 inflicted a defeat on the Austrians, who lost around 38,000 men compared to just 10,000 French.

The victory did Napoleon little good, for while he was at Dresden, Marshal MacDonald, with the main French body advancing against the Prussians, had been too enthusiastic in his drive to pin down the enemy and suffered a heavy defeat when Blücher had turned on him. MacDonald's rashness cost Napoleon another 15,000 men and 100 cannon. Napoleon also learnt that his former marshal Bernadotte, now Crown Prince of Sweden, was bearing down on his flank – just as the Allies had planned. A further 60,000 Russians also made their appearance on the Elbe. The Coalition forces were becoming stronger as Napoleon's were becoming weaker.

The Battle of the Nations

Napoleon took up a position at Leipzig which can be reflected on in two different ways. Either it placed him in a central position from which he could operate with favourable interior lines against the encircling Coalition armies, or it could be viewed that he was all-but surrounded by the enemy. It was certainly the latter view that Blücher took. 'The three armies [Prussian, Austrian and Russian; the Swedes still being some distance behind the Prussians] are now so close together,' he wrote on 13 October, 'that a simultaneous attack, against the point where the enemy has concentrated his forces, might be undertaken'.[3] ➢

Austrian troops in camp prior to the Battle of Leipzig. In the foreground, surrounded by his staff, Feldmarschall Karl Philipp, Prince Schwarzenberg, the commander-in-chief of the allied Grand Army of Bohemia, can be seen handing a despatch to an Uhlan. (Anne S.K. Brown Military Collection, Brown University Library)

Battle Of The Nations ⚜ Napoleon Bonaparte

ABOVE: *The retreat of Napoleon's forces underway on 19 October 1813. The disastrously mistimed demolition of the bridge, which trapped thousands of men on the wrong side of the River Elster, can be seen.*

Napoleon, likewise, saw the prospect of an imminent battle and he concentrated as many men as he could at Leipzig. By 15 October, he had almost 180,000 under his direct command with more on their way, so by the 16th, the day of the greatest battle of the Napoleonic Wars, he had amassed a force of around 225,000 men. The Allies, though, had more, far more, being able to count around 380,000 of all ranks. A staggering total of 600,000 men would fight to the death in and around the ancient Saxon city.

Napoleon planned to hold the Allies to the north of Leipzig and then deliver a massive blow, with five army corps and the Imperial Guard, on their eastern flank. He did not expect there to be much action to the west and consequently had not arranged for any additional bridges to be constructed over either the River Pleiss or the River Elster.

For their part, the Allies aimed to sweep round the marshes to the south of Leipzig, but when the battle began at 06.30 hours on 16 October, they found that the French had already moved their forces in that direction. Equally, Napoleon was surprised to find Blücher's men bearing down from the north, but the main action to the south-east went well for the French, as Schwarzenberg's Austrian Army of Bohemia and Bennigsen's Russians battled with Napoleon's main force, which included a 150-gun battery which pounded the Austrian front. After halting the Austrian attack, Napoleon launched what he believed would be his knock-out blow.

During this time Marshal Marmont's corps was facing the full weight of Blücher's army. Somehow, he had to hold out until his Emperor had defeated the Austrians. This Marmot achieved in wonderful fashion, and as darkness brought an end to the fighting, he could proudly claim to have held the Prussians at bay all day.

Napoleon, however, had failed to destroy the Austro-Russian forces. Schwarzenberg's and Bennigsen's attack had indeed been beaten back in disarray, but Napoleon had failed to follow up his initial success and the arrival of reinforcements allowed the Allies to mount a counter-attack and recover the ground they had lost. Day one of the battle had seen neither side gain the upper hand.

Both sides paused for breath during the 17th with only a couple of small-scale actions. But it was on that day that Napoleon learnt of the arrival of further Allied reinforcements, including Bernadotte's Swedes and even a troop of British Horse Artillery armed with rockets. He now knew that he was facing more than 300,000 men, even after taking into account the losses of the day before. He knew he could not prevail against such numbers. The Coalition generals had, meanwhile, used the 17th to plan a converging attack upon Leipzig, aiming to crush Napoleon.

ABOVE: *Among those who lost their lives attempting to cross the river was Maréchal d'Empire Prince Józef Antoni Poniatowski who, badly injured from the fighting at Leipzig, drowned. This engraving depicts his efforts to try and escape Coalition soldiers, a retreating soldier in the foreground trying to rescue him.* (Anne S.K. Brown Military Collection, Brown University Library)

BELOW: *A panoramic painting by Alexander Zaureweid of the Battle of Leipzig, 16-19 October 1813.*

The Bridge Over The Elster

Napoleon pulled his troops back to concentrate their strength as much as possible, and planned for a retreat on the 18th if necessary. When the fighting recommenced on the 18th with the Allies attacking in confident fashion, the situation become even worse for Napoleon, as two brigades of Saxon troops and some from the other German state of Württemberg deserted to the Allies – a total of 12,000 men and forty-two guns.[4]

In a dogged defensive duel, the French held on throughout the 18th, and during the night began their withdrawal. All went fairly smoothly until they reached the River Elster. A corporal of engineers had been instructed to demolish the bridge over the river after the last of the French troops had crossed. But he panicked when he saw Prussian cavalry appear and he ignited the mines which had been laid whilst there were still tens of thousands of French troops who had not crossed the river.

The original caption states that this painting depicts 'a Prussian dragoon and French infantry in battle near edge of brook or creek', during the Battle of Leipzig. It is possible that the artist has depicted the fate of some of the thousands of French soldiers trapped by the demolition of the bridge over the River Elster. (Anne S.K. Brown Military Collection, Brown University Library)

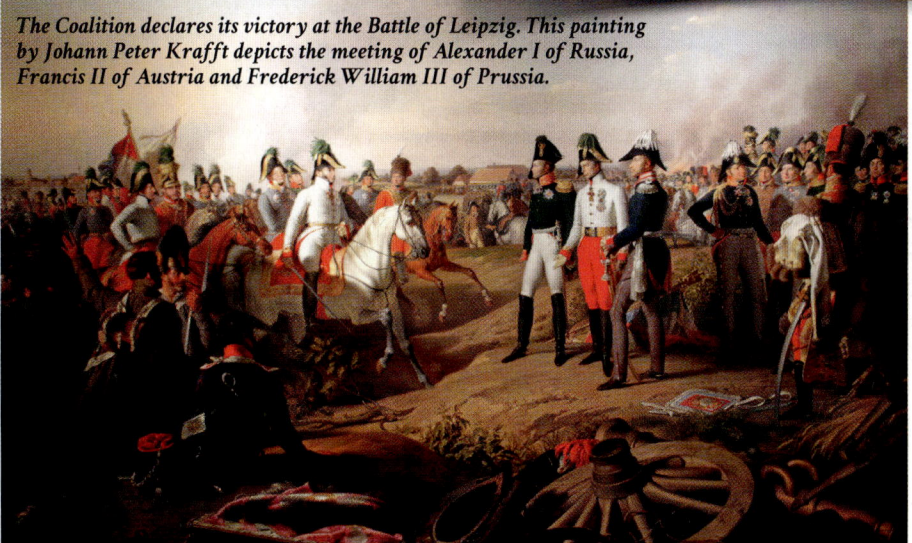

The Coalition declares its victory at the Battle of Leipzig. This painting by Johann Peter Krafft depicts the meeting of Alexander I of Russia, Francis II of Austria and Frederick William III of Prussia.

'One can imagine the despair of these brave soldiers, gathered on the bank of a deep river with the entire coalition army at their heels,' wrote Colonel Noël. 'They had no alternatives other than to throw themselves into the water and attempt to swim across the Elster, to be massacred in an attempt to defend themselves, or to surrender. Many were drowned, a large number were slain in a useless resistance, and others were forced to lay down their arms.'[5] Possibly as many as 20,000 men, and the entire artillery train of one corps, was lost because of this blunder.

All that Napoleon could do was to try and get his army back to France and rebuild once more, hopeless as this must inevitably be. As with the retreat from Moscow, order was soon lost.

'We marched at will, confused, driven on, pitilessly crushed, abandoned without succour,' recalled one officer of the Imperial Guard. 'We arrived on the banks of the Rhine [on 2 November] as we left the banks of the Elster, in a state of complete dissolution. We had covered our track with the relics of our army. At every step we took we left behind us corpses of men and carcases of horses, guns, baggage, tatters of our one-time glory. It was a horrible spectacle, that wrung the heart with agony. To all these woes combined were added yet others that further aggravated our grievous situation – typhus broke out in our disorganised ranks in a terrifying fashion.'[6]

Napoleon returned to Paris, as he had less than twelve months earlier, to raise another army from the ashes of one he had lost. 'One year ago, all Europe marched with us,' he told the Senate at the Tuileries on 14 November. 'Today all of Europe marches against us.'[7]

It was essentially true. This was because the mood had changed in Europe. Sparked by the unquenchable nationalism of the guerrillas in Spain and the sacrificial patriotism of the Russians, the armies that Napoleon now faced were no longer the weapons of the old monarchies, they were peoples' armies. For too long the French soldiers had transported not the ideals of the Revolution, but had stolen and scavenged. War was an expensive business, and from the Directory to the Empire, war had to pay for war, and it was the countries through which the French armies travelled or where they had placed their garrisons that did the paying. Napoleon famously remarked that 'an army marches on its stomach' and the unprecedented speed at which his armies marched was due, in no small measure, to abandoning unwieldly and slow supply trains, relying on his men to find food from the fields and the towns through which they passed. When this was not possible, as he saw in Russia, his army starved. ➤

ABOVE: *The victors enter Leipzig on 19 October 1813 – a scene that shows the 'grand entry of the allied sovereigns' into the city, 'Austrian and Russian infantry lining sides of square and holding back crowds cheering'.* (Anne S.K. Brown Military Collection, Brown University Library)

BATTLE OF THE NATIONS — NAPOLEON BONAPARTE

A watercolour depicting Napoleon, sat in a shelter with his head on his hand, during the retreat from Leipzig. (Anne S.K. Brown Military Collection, Brown University Library)

Europe had had enough. It was time to be done with all the fighting and the dying. It was time to be done with Napoleon.

The Invasion of France

On 1 January 1814, Blücher's combined Russo-Prussian army poured over the border into France, to Napoleon's complete surprise. He could scarcely believe that anyone would dare invade France. But already the Austrians had marched into Switzerland and other Coalition armies had entered the Low Countries and were bearing down on the Rhine.

Napoleon immediately ordered a *levee en masse* in the eastern Departments of France. The young conscripts, responding to an appeal from Napoleon's loyal Queen Marie Louise, were nicknamed 'Marie Louises'. But for all their patriotic fervour, they were ill-used by the Emperor. Half-trained, half-clothed and half-fed, they were destined to be slaughtered.

As always, Napoleon thought only of the offensive and he marshalled his forces to attack the enemy, leaving his wife in Paris as regent, declaring that, 'she is wiser than all my ministers'.[8] The defence of Paris, however, was entrusted to his brother Joseph, who had been ejected from Spain by the Duke of Wellington. Joseph had demonstrated a complete lack of martial ability in the Peninsula, yet Napoleon was clearly worried about the political situation in the French capital and he knew he could rely on his own family to keep any dissident voices muted.

Napoleon left Paris on 23 January 1814 and four days later attacked Blücher close to Brienne-le-Château (where it might be recalled that the nine-year-old Napoleon had his first taste of military training), using his standard practice of holding the enemy centre while he delivered the telling blow from the flank. This resulted in a victory for the Emperor, which saw Blücher lose 4,000 men. But it was a comparatively small affair, with Blücher, in his enthusiasm forgetting the policies of the Trachenberg Plan, having marched ahead of the other Coalition armies.

Blücher, though, would not give up, and after being joined by Austrians, Bavarians and Württembergers, he faced Napoleon again at La Rothière on 1 February 1814. With the augmentation of his force, Blücher had almost twice as many men as Napoleon, and the Emperor was forced to retreat.

This was merely the prelude to a worsening situation, as tens of thousands of new recruits deserted the colours. Napoleon had lost his magnetic appeal.

Buried Under The Ruins

At the height of Napoleon's power, those around him had bathed luxuriantly in the reflected glory. To all who followed him were honours, titles and wealth. Now, he could offer them nothing other than the chance to die for France. It held little appeal.

Napoleon knew that the end was nigh, writing to his brother Joseph on 12 January that, 'No preparations are to be made for abandoning Paris; if necessary we must be buried under its ruins'. By 8 February his defiance had changed to one of acceptance, this time writing, 'If news should come of a lost battle and my death … Send the Empress and the King of Rome [their son] to [the Château of] Rambouillet [a royal residence to the south-west of Paris]. Never let the Empress or the King of Rome fall into the hands of the enemy. I feel I would rather my son was strangled, than see him brought up in Vienna as an Austrian prince.'[9] That, though, is exactly what would happen, and he would be joined by his mother in Vienna.

As for Napoleon, his fate now hung in the balance, as the Coalition armies bore down on Paris. ❖

ABOVE: *The imposing Monument to the Battle of the Nations in south-east Leipzig. Paid for mostly by donations and funds raised by the city of Leipzig, the memorial was completed in 1913 to mark the 100th anniversary of the battle. It was constructed at a cost of six million goldmarks. Some 300 feet tall, a climb of over 500 steps takes the visitor to a viewing platform at the top, from which there are views across the city and environs. (Shutterstock)*

NOTES:
1. David Chandler, *The Campaigns of Napoleon* (Macmillan, New York, 1966), p.853.
2. So named for the conference held at the palace of Trachenberg in Silesia.
3. Quoted in Chandler, p.922.
4. This is the figure given by Colonel Jean-Nicolas-Auguste Noël in *With Napoleon's Guns, The Military Memoirs of an Officer of the First Empire* (Frontline, Barnsley, 2016), p.184.
5. ibid, p.187.
6. Jean-Baptise Barrès, *Memoirs of a French Napoleonic Officer* (Frontline, Barnsley, 2017), pp.197-8.
7. R.M. Johnston, *In the Words of Napoleon, The Emperor Day by Day* (Frontline, Barnsley, 2015), p.283.
8. Digby Smith, *The Decline and Fall of Napoleon's Empire, How the Emperor Self-Destructed* (Frontline, Barnsley, 2015), p.171.
9. ibid, p.174.

NAPOLEON BONAPARTE — ABDICATION AND EXILE

Abdication And Exile

There was to be no heroic last stand in Paris; there would be no ruins under which the Bonapartes would die fighting. In the end, the fall of Napoleon's empire was quite peaceful and even civilised.

In what was called the 'Six Days' Campaign', Napoleon demonstrated just why he was a master in the art of warfare. Facing multiple enemies, he struck with lightning speed, first on an isolated Russian division at Champaubert on 10 February 1814, and then on a combined Russo-Prussian corps under generals von Yorck and Sacken at Monmirail the next day. Again, on 12 February, he caught the Army of Silesia and defeated the Russians and Prussians at Château-Thierry, and yet again two days later at Vauchamps, where von Kleist's II Prussian Corps and the Russian X Corps were beaten, the Coalition forces losing almost 3,500 men. On 17 February, he defeated the Austrians at Nangis, following this up with another success at Montereau on the Seine the next day.

Brilliant, though, this all was, such efforts were in vain. There were simply too many Coalition armies advancing on Paris for Napoleon's dwindling band to hold back – and the tables began to turn.

Wherever Napoleon was not present in person, the French armies were defeated, or surrendered. Even more disturbing for Napoleon were the rumours from Paris where it was said, plans were already being made for a time when Napoleon was no longer head of state.

Yet Napoleon doubted the Allies would have the temerity to attempt the capture of the French capital. But they would not need to do that to bring about his downfall.

The Island of Elba

As the Coalition armies pressed ever closer to Paris, four of Napoleon's surviving marshals, including Ney, whom the Emperor had called 'the bravest of the brave', demanded Napoleon's abdication to save the nation's capital from destruction. Napoleon refused, declaring he would continue to fight and that the army would follow him. To this, Ney replied with the immortal words: 'No it will not. The army will obey its commanders!' Napoleon knew at that moment his valiant struggle against his enemies was over.

As the allied powers had declared that it was not France they were fighting but Napoleon himself, he agreed to abdicate. However, Napoleon, still hoping that the Bonaparte

LEFT: *Napoleon confirms the details of his abdication by signing the Treaty of Fontainebleau on 11 April 1814.*

ABDICATION AND EXILE NAPOLEON BONAPARTE

With all the details of his abdication settled at the Treaty of Fontainebleau on 11 April 1814, Napoleon left for Elba on 20 April 1814.

'Farewell My Children!'

His departure from the Courtyard of the White Horse in the Tuileries was a moving and memorable event. As the moment came, General Jean-Martin Petit, commander of the 1st Grenadiers of the Old Guard, the army's senior regiment, ordered his men to present arms. The drums began to beat as regime would continue to reign in France, abdicated in favour of his three-year-old son. Understandably, this offer was rejected by the Coalition parties, who demanded unconditional acceptance of their demands. Napoleon was powerless to object.

The allies were surprisingly generous in the terms that they offered Napoleon. He would be exiled to the Mediterranean island of Elba which would become a separate principality ruled by Napoleon. He would be allowed to retain his title of Emperor and Elba would have its own independence. He was also granted an annual pension of 2 million francs and was permitted to take with him a retinue of 600 persons. His wife and other members of his family were also granted substantial pensions.

ABOVE: *Napoleon, seen here at the head of his marshals and staff, leads his men over roads made muddy by days of rain. Though his empire was crumbling, Napoleon proved to be a dangerous opponent in the Six Days Campaign.*

BELOW: *One of the engagements fought during the Six Days Campaign, in this case the Battle of Monmirail on 11 February 1814.*

ABOVE: *A contemporary satirical cartoon celebrating Napoleon's exile to Elba. A joyful procession accompanies Napoleon, looking forlorn and bedraggled, to the boat which would transport him to Elba. Napoleon, in the centre, is shown wearing his uniform coat backwards with his hands tied behind his back. Large tears drip from his eyes while a small demon fiddles and dances on his head.* (Anne S.K. Brown Military Collection, Brown University Library)

Napoleon Bonaparte — Abdication and Exile

ABOVE: *Officers and guards lead Napoleon to an armoured carriage, the start of his journey into exile.* (Anne S.K. Brown Military Collection, Brown University Library)

the Emperor appeared on the stairs, wearing the uniform coat of the chasseurs of the Guard, with blue breeches, top boots, and his legendary hat. The grooms stood by the carriages, with General Lefebvre-Desnoëttes on horseback at the head of the escort of 1,500 Old Guard troopers.

The trumpets blew a loud fanfare as the Emperor descended the stairs and shook hands with Petit who moved forward to meet him. Then Napoleon walked to the centre of the court: 'Officers, non-commissioned officers and soldiers of my Old Guard, I bid you farewell. For twenty years I have been pleased with you. I have always found you on the path to glory. The Allied Powers have armed all of Europe against me. Part of the army has betrayed its trust – and France. Now that another destiny lies in store for her. I must sacrifice my most cherished interests. With you and the brave men who have remained loyal I could have continued the war for three years; but France would have suffered, which was contrary to my purpose. Be loyal to the new ruler whom France has chosen. Never abandon this dear country that has suffered so long.

'Do not pity my fate. I shall be happy so long as I know that you are happy … Now I shall write the story of what we have done.'

At those words, Petit waved his sword in the air and cried, '*Vive l'Empereur!* which was echoed by the whole Guard.

'I cannot embrace you all,' Napoleon continued, 'but I shall embrace your general'. He embraced Petit then called for the Guard's

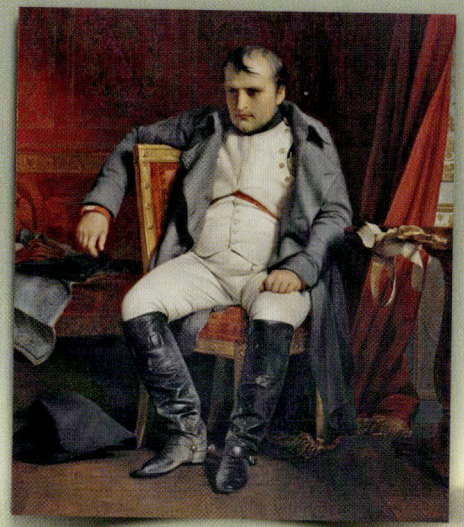

ABOVE: *Facing the inevitable, on 4 April 1814, Napoleon abdicated in favour of his son, with Marie Louise as regent – the day that he is depicted in this portrait of him at Fontainebleau by Paul Delaroche.*

eagle to be taken to him. He held it and kissed it three times: 'Dear eagle, let my embrace echo in the hearts of these brave men. 'Farewell, my children.'[1]

As the cheers echoed round the courtyard, Napoleon mounted his carriage and set off, surrounded, for the final time, by the duty squadron of the chasseurs à cheval.

Captain Jean Coignet also watched the poignant ceremony, admitting that it was 'a heart-rending moment. Groans came from all up and down the ranks, and, I must confess that I shed tears when I saw my dear Emperor start for the island of Elba.'[2]

It was the end of the dream, a glorious but impossible dream, to spread the ideals of the Revolution to the rest of Europe. But Europe was not ready for such change and the old monarchies, Britain more than any other, would not stop fighting until Napoleon was driven from power and the pompous, powdered Bourbons were back on the throne of France.

In reality, the dream was only that of one man, and with that man condemned to exile, Europe could look forward to peace after twenty years of conflict that had seen between 5 and 7 million people, military and civilian, lose their lives. ❖

NOTES:
1. Henry Lahouque and A.S.K. Brown, *The Anatomy of Glory, Napoleon and his Guard* (Frontline, Barnsley), pp.420-1.
2. Captain Jean-Roch Coignet, *The Note-Books of Captain Coignet, Soldier of the Empire, 1799-1816* (Frontline, Barnsley, 2016), p.267.

KEY Military ▶ THE ONLINE HOME OF...

CLASSIC MILITARY VEHICLE

BRITAIN AT WAR — A HISTORY OF CONFLICT

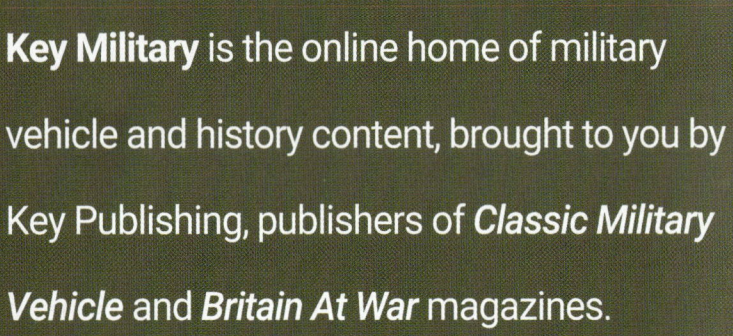

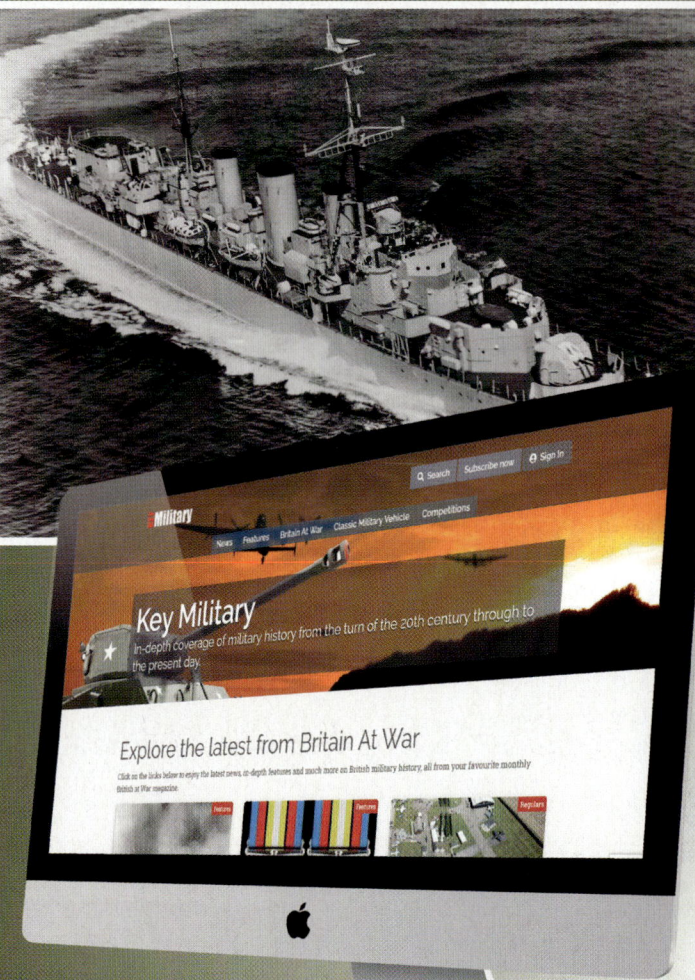

Key Military is the online home of military vehicle and history content, brought to you by Key Publishing, publishers of *Classic Military Vehicle* and *Britain At War* magazines.

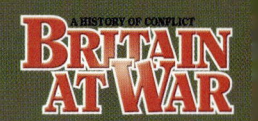

keymilitary.com

You'll find an array of content on Key Military – including latest news, in-depth features and online exclusives.

UNLIMITED access to this exciting online content from our dedicated team starts from just £29.99/year for UK customers. And registering couldn't be simpler - for instant access to the latest *Classic Military Vehicle* and *Britain At War* Magazine features and industry-leading content, just visit www.keymilitary.com/subscribe.

FREE ACCESS

FOR ALL SUBSCRIBERS* TO...

CLASSIC MILITARY VEHICLE

BRITAIN AT WAR — A HISTORY OF CONFLICT

VISIT
keymilitary.com/subscribe

*Free access available for a limited time only

SIGN UP TODAY!

We value your feedback! Let us know your thoughts on Key Military – drop us a line at subs@keypublishing.com today

Return of the Eagles – Waterloo

The magical story of the young Corsican who rose to be an emperor and the most powerful man in Europe is one of the greatest of all time. Yet, there was to be a postscript, which culminated in one of the most memorable battles in history.

Possibly, if Napoleon had been treated with respect by Louis XVIII, who had been restored to the throne of France, and his legacy cherished, the Emperor might have remained in gilded exile on Elba and, as he had promised, written his memoirs. But his army was disbanded somewhat ignominiously, with thousands of officers and men – the great heroes of the Empire – left with neither status nor income. Equally, Napoleon was not provided with the promised funds to support himself and his retinue on Elba. It seemed that the great triumphs of the Empire counted for nothing and that the Revolution, and everything Napoleon and his men had achieved, was an aberration best forgotten.

With peace, thousands had been made unemployed with the closure of clothing and equipment factories that had been established to supply the army. In addition, the Napoleonic state had required a huge bureaucracy to function, and with the change of government many hundreds of pen-pushers were without work; those jobs that had existed for the men who had served the state (in many cases for over a decade) found their posts being given to returning royalists. Economic hardships were not helped by the new government levying heavy taxation to put money back into the government's coffers. France was virtually bankrupt and to save money the army, now on a peace footing, had jettisoned thousands of men who now flooded onto the labour market. The winter of 1814-15 was certainly one of discontent across much of France.

A contemplative Napoleon on the shore of the Island of Elba. (Anne S.K. Brown Military Collection, Brown University Library)

Return Of The Eagles - Waterloo Napoleon Bonaparte

The scene at Porto Ferrajo, Elba, during Napoleon's departure on 26 February 1815. (Musée Naval et Napoléonien du Cap d'Antibes)

Napoleon was aware of the mood in France and believed that if he returned from exile, he would be welcomed by the majority of the people. So, with his not insignificant retinue, which had swollen a little beyond the numbers he had been permitted to take to Elba, he slipped away from Porto Ferrajo on 26 February 1815 to embark on what was unquestionably the greatest gamble of his life. With just 1,100 men, he was going to invade France.

Enemy of the World

Napoleon landed on the south coast of France between Cannes and Antibes, and started on the march to Paris. All along the route, Napoleon was cheered by the people. His first real challenge came at Laffrey, near Grenoble, where his route was blocked by the French 5th Regiment of the Line. The opposing forces levelled their muskets. But Napoleon stepped forward. He threw open his coat and offered his breast to the Bourbon troops.

'If any of you will shoot your Emperor,' he declared, 'shoot him now'.

The order to fire was given, but not a single shot rang out. The men threw down their muskets and flocked round him. From that moment on the march to Paris become more like a procession, as all the forces sent out by King Louis to stop Napoleon simply fell in behind him. Napoleon entered Paris on 20 March 1815, just hours after Louis had fled.

A view of Forte Stella and Napoleon's residence on the island of Elba – the latter is the large yellow building just below and to the left of the lighthouse. Two plaques on the building's wall inform visitors of its one-time resident. There are, in fact, at least three buildings on the island that were used by Napoleon, two of which served as summer and winter palaces. (Shutterstock)

Napoleon Bonaparte — Return Of The Eagles - Waterloo

Despite all the support he had received, Napoleon knew that his people did not want to become embroiled in another war. He also knew that Europe was weary of fighting. All he sought, therefore, was to be recognised by the other nations as the *de facto* ruler of France. If the Allied governments would let him sit peacefully on the French throne there need be no more bloodshed. However, all his peace efforts were ignored and just five days after he had reinstalled himself in the Tuileries, the great powers of Europe formed the Seventh Coalition, not against France, but against Napoleon himself, who was described by them as the 'disturber of the tranquillity of the world'.

The Allied powers, whose representatives had been attempting to reach agreement on the future nature of Europe at the Congress of Vienna, quickly decided to assemble a force of more than 700,000 men to defeat Napoleon. Whatever course of action Napoleon embarked upon, his destiny was decided, for he could not possibly beat the combined strength of his enemies.

Napoleon onboard L'Inconstant during his return from Elba, having been on the island for 300 days. (Anne S.K. Brown Military Collection, Brown University Library)

Napoleon's journey from Golfe-Juan to Paris is famous as the Route Napoléon and is still marked as such to this day. It is now a 325-kilometre section of the Route Nationale 85. This picture shows a gilded eagle marker of the Route Napoléon which can be seen at the southern entry to the town of Gap, the capital of the Hautes-Alpes department. (Courtesy of Fr. Latreille)

Now fully cognisant that he would have to fight to save his crown, Napoleon set to work with all his old energy. Conscription was reintroduced in late April, but it would be months before these new troops could be trained and equipped. What he would have to fight the Allied armies with would be the old soldiers of 1814. At the most, including all the Bourbon army and those men who had been pushed into retirement, France would be able to muster just 300,000 experienced soldiers – less than half that of the Coalition.

The Duke of Wellington

Knowing that he would have to fight, Napoleon then had to decide whether to wait around Paris whilst his army grew in strength, hoping that the Allies would be sluggish in their mobilisation, or should he strike at the enemy forces already gathering in Belgium close to the French border? If, indeed, he could attack into Belgium and achieve a stunning victory, its impact might induce the former French-controlled parts of what had just recently become the Kingdom of the United Netherlands to abandon the Coalition and rally to the Tricolour. Many in the Netherlands army had once fought under the Imperial Eagle and might be persuaded to again. Such a victory might also cause dissent and division in the ranks of the Allies.

The man given charge of the Anglo-Netherlands army was the Duke of Wellington who, following his unbroken run of victories in Portugal and Spain, was regarded as the finest of the Allied generals.

Napoleon had never crossed swords with Wellington. Now might be the time to show the world just who was the most brilliant commander. The defeat of Wellington would send shock waves throughout Europe. If Napoleon was to hold onto his throne, sooner or later, he had to beat the Duke of Wellington, and sooner would be better.

On 4 April 1815, Wellington arrived in Belgium to take up his new post. What he found cannot have been very inspiring. His army included the Dutch and Belgian troops of the United Netherlands plus various regiments of Hanoverian militia, the British King George still being also the Elector of Hanover. He had comparatively few British regiments. The Duke of Brunswick, brother-in-law of the Prince Regent, added a small contingent, as did the German Dutchy of

The brig L'Inconstant, ferrying Napoleon to France, crosses the path of the brig Zéphir during the journey. L'Inconstant flies the Tricolour of the Empire, while Zéphir flies the white ensign of the French Monarchy. Soldiers of the Imperial Guard are depicted crouching on deck while Napoleon stands fore of the main mast. This painting was ordered by Napoleon himself, with Captain Taillade (of L'Inconstant) being instructed to provide the artist, Ambroise-Louis Garneray, with all the information and assistance required for its completion. (Musée National de la Marine)

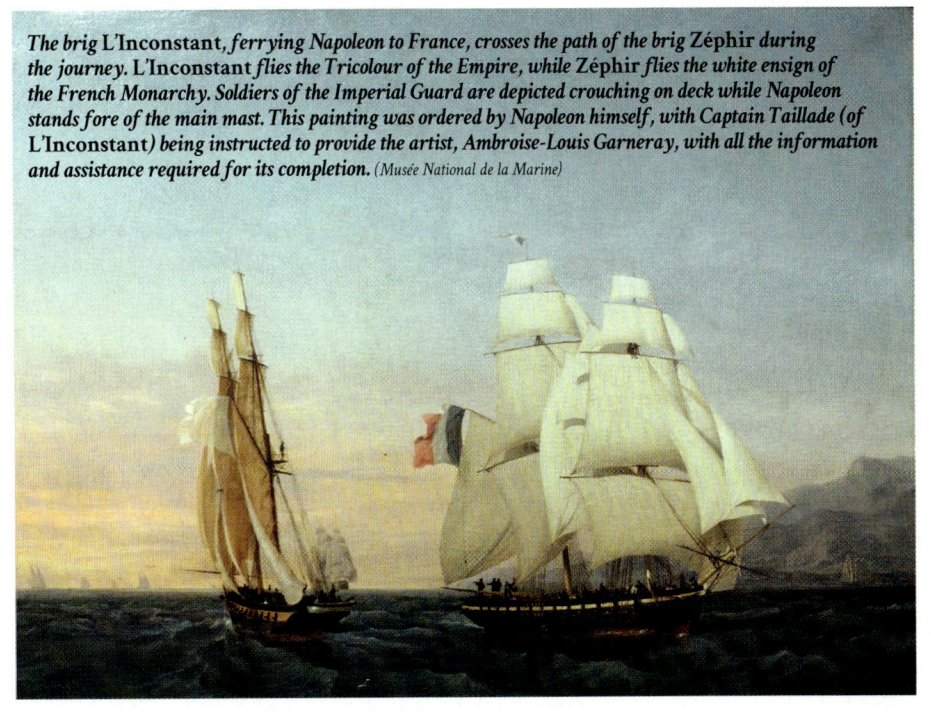

89

RETURN OF THE EAGLES - WATERLOO NAPOLEON BONAPARTE

Napoleon, on the right, landed in the Bay of Golfe-Juan, near Antibes, on 1 March 1815.
(Anne S.K. Brown Military Collection, Brown University Library)

Nassau. Altogether, Wellington's mixed force numbered just under 90,000 men, which rose to 107,000 before hostilities began.

This force was not the only one in Belgium facing the French, for on the border with the German states was Blücher's Prussian army of 128,000 men. This made a combined Allied force more than 200,000 strong.

'Napoleon Has Humbugged Me, By God!'

Wellington believed that together, he and Blücher were strong enough to take on and defeat Napoleon without waiting for the Austrians and the Russians. He calculated that the longer the Allies waited the stronger Napoleon would become. He wanted, therefore, to invade France at the soonest opportunity. But before he could make the move he envisaged, Napoleon struck.

On the morning of 15 June, the leading elements of Napoleon's Armée du Nord crossed the River Sambre and fell on the Prussian outposts. News of this was sent to both Wellington and Blücher. Wellington expected Napoleon to advance further to the west where he could threaten the British army's communications with the Channel ports, and he dismissed the move by the French as a diversion.

Though Wellington decided to wait for more definite information regarding Napoleon's direction of attack, the Chief-of-Staff of the Netherlands Army, Jean Baron de Constant Rebecque, respond immediately by sending a brigade to occupy the key crossroads at Quatre Bras. This action saved Wellington from catastrophe for Napoleon had placed his army in between the Prussians and the British. Wellington was totally unprepared for this. He could not imagine that Napoleon would place his army right in the very centre of the Allied positions. All Napoleon had to do now was drive the two Allied armies apart so that he could concentrate all his strength on each one in turn. He sent one wing of his army under Marshal Ney to take and hold Quatre Bras and hold back Wellington, while he delivered his main assault upon the Prussians. But when Ney arrived at Quatre Bras he found it was already held by the Dutch and he did not press home an attack. Rebecque had bought Wellington a few hours' grace.

Wellington was at the famous Duke of Richmond's ball in Brussels when he received

Napoleon being greeted by the men of the 5th Regiment at Grenoble, 7 March 1815, after his escape from Elba.

Napoleon Bonaparte — Return Of The Eagles - Waterloo

Bowing to the inevitable, Louis XVIII left Paris at midnight on 19 March 1815. (Anne S.K. Brown Military Collection, Brown University Library)

a message from the Dutch which confirmed that Napoleon had indeed split the Coalition armies apart. 'Napoleon has humbugged me, by God!' Wellington is reputed to have exclaimed. 'He has gained twenty-four hours' march on me.'

Wellington asked the Duke of Richmond for a map. He told Richmond that he would be unable to stop Napoleon at Quatre Bras, 'so, I must fight him here', at the same time pointing with his thumb along the map, just below a small village called … Waterloo.

Quatre Bras and Ligny

Having finally appreciated the seriousness of the situation he had been placed in by Napoleon's bold move, Wellington acted swiftly, ordering his troops to march with all speed to Quatre Bras which was still held by the small Dutch force. It is often said that Ney acted uncharacteristically cautiously on 15 June and had he attacked Quatre Bras with all the troops at his disposal he could have taken the crossroads before Wellington's troops arrived.

Yet Ney had only just joined the Armée du Nord, and he had, therefore, been excluded from the planning of the campaign and not all the corps commanders whom Ney was given authority over were aware of his presence in the field. He was not in a position to attack Quatre Bras on the 15th, but as the body of troops holding the crossroads was small, Ney was confident that he would be able to capture Quatre Bras the next morning. But he was wrong, for by the time Ney had assembled a strong enough force to mount a serious attack upon the crossroads, the first of Wellington's regiments had marched up from Brussels. Ney found himself facing almost the entire Anglo-Netherlands army.

Meanwhile, Napoleon had concentrated the rest of his army on the Prussians, and had brought them to battle seven miles to the east at the village of Ligny. In a brutal encounter, the Prussians were defeated, losing around 20,000 men, including many who deserted. Napoleon, however, failed to achieve the crushing victory which was essential for his plan to work. This was, in part, due to a shocking mix-up for which Napoleon was entirely to blame.

Ney received a message from Napoleon instructing him to 'beat and destroy all the enemy corps which may present themselves' at Quatre Bras. But while Ney was in the process of attacking Wellington at Quatre Bras, he received another message from Napoleon telling him to 'manoeuvre immediately in such a manner as to envelop the enemy's [the Prussians] right and fall upon his rear; the army in our front is lost if you act with energy … The fate of France is in your hands. Do not hesitate even for a moment.'[1]

What was Ney to do? He could not be in two places at once. He decided that all he could do

Napoleon addresses the Old Guard as it prepares to attack the Allied centre at Waterloo.

was defeat Wellington as quickly as possible and then go to help Napoleon. But Napoleon, seeing his chance of destroying the Prussians slipping away, and without informing Ney, ordered d'Erlon's I Corps, which was part of Ney's command, to march on Ligny instead of Quatre Bras.

When Ney received a note from d'Erlon advising him that he had been instructed by the Emperor to march on Ligny, Ney was furious. How could he beat Wellington with half of his infantry strength taken from him?

Ney countermanded Napoleon's instructions and told d'Erlon to return to Quatre Bras immediately. By the time he received Ney's order, d'Erlon was in sight of Ligny, but he turned back as ordered. I Corps did not reach Quatre Bras until nightfall. Indeed, I Corps spent 16 June marching backwards and forwards between the two battlefields without firing a shot. The result was that Ney was unable to wrest control of Quatre Bras from Wellington, and Napoleon's victory over the Prussians was not conclusive. ➢

Napoleon on the Waterloo battlefield, his left hand resting on a broken fence-post or palisade, with wounded in foreground. (Anne S.K. Brown Military Collection, Brown University Library)

Return Of The Eagles - Waterloo Napoleon Bonaparte

Another depiction of Napoleon, mounted, departing from the Waterloo battlefield, making way through mass of retreating soldiers, wounded and dead. (Anne S.K. Brown Military Collection, Brown University Library)

This was the first serious error that Napoleon made which cost him the campaign, and he was about to make a second, and even more disastrous one.

Though Wellington still held Quatre Bras, the Prussians had been forced to retreat to avoid destruction. Blücher himself was hurt in the disorderly retreat and if Napoleon would have pursued the beaten enemy vigorously the Prussians might have been unable to rally and no longer play an active part in the campaign. But it was not until 11.00 hours on the morning of 17 June that Napoleon ordered Marshal Grouchy to take almost a third of the Armée du Nord and pursue the Prussians.

The Prussians had been allowed the whole of the night of the 16th/17th and all the following morning to reorganise themselves. Grouchy, try as he might, would always be behind the Prussians, while the advance elements of Blücher's army marched without interference to join up with Wellington. With his swift initial advance, Napoleon had separated the two Allied armies, but his inexplicable delay in pursuing the Prussians on 16 June allowed them to reunite. This would mean that when Napoleon fought again on 18 June he would be facing both Wellington and Blücher.

The Throw of the Dice

Though Wellington had held Quatre Bras, because the Prussians had been forced to retreat, he also had to fall back to avoid being outflanked. He withdrew during the 17th to the position he had already earmarked – the ridge of Mont St Jean to the south of the village of Waterloo.

Napoleon followed up the Anglo-Netherlands army and by the morning of 18 June 1815, his army was drawn up in battle array. At around 11.30 hours the culminating battle of the Napoleonic Wars began.

Wellington had posted his troops north of a track which passed along a low ridge. Described as a 'sunken road', troops stationed along the road were well protected from enemy fire. Ahead of the ridge were three significant buildings which had been turned into strongpoints – the Château d'Hougoumont on the right, the farmhouse of

A coloured lithograph of a battle scene depicting the last stand of the Imperial Guard. Napoleon can be seen on a horse in the background. (Anne S.K. Brown Military Collection, Brown University Library)

NAPOLEON BONAPARTE   RETURN OF THE EAGLES - WATERLOO

Napoleon leaves the battlefield to escape in his carriage. (Anne S.K. Brown Military Collection, Brown University Library)

La Haye Sainte in the centre, where the road from Charleroi ran up and over the ridge, and to the left were the farms of Papelotte and La Haye. The entire Allied line, composed of 67,661 men, was less than two miles long.

The bulk of Wellington's army was below the crest of the ridge and therefore largely hidden from Napoleon's view across the low valley to the south. Napoleon, therefore, had to plan his attack on assumptions rather than facts. What he did know was that there was a distinct possibility that Grouchy might be unable to prevent Blücher reaching Waterloo. The Emperor, whose army was only slightly larger than Wellington's, at around 72,000 men, knew he had to defeat the British before the Prussians arrived.

His attack began with a diversionary assault upon Hougoumont. This was followed by a fierce bombardment of the centre of Wellington's line before his infantry was launched against the Mont St Jean.

Every French attack was driven off, though it was, by Wellington's own admission, a 'close run thing'. The British commander knew that unless the Prussians joined him, he might well suffer his first defeat. But by mid-afternoon, much earlier than most people realise, the Prussian IV Corps was already making its presence felt on the French right. Napoleon had to send increasing numbers of regiments to shore up his right flank, as the Prussians steadily advanced.

Napoleon knew that he had to break Wellington soon, or be crushed between the two Allied armies. In one last throw of the dice, he placed himself at the head of eight battalions of his Guard, and led them towards Wellington's centre. Wellington watched as they approached to where the British Brigade of Guards was waiting in the sunken lane. At the critical moment, the Guards rose up and delivered a devastating volley. With another battalion, the 52nd, wheeling round to pour fire into the flank of the French column, the Imperial Guard was decimated.

Napoleon's Guard fell back. Soon the chilling news that the Guard had been defeated spread throughout the French ranks, and the rest of Napoleon's army took to its collective heels. The Emperor's army disintegrated. Though total French casualties are usually given as in excess of 40,000 – almost double that of the Anglo-Netherlands army – recent research which has uncovered French casualty returns and British prisoner of war records, reveals that most of the French losses were through desertion.[2] The soldiers of France no longer believed in Napoleon and they saw no point in sacrificing themselves for a lost cause. ❖

NOTES:
1. William Seymour, Eberhard Kaulbach and Jacques Champagne, *Waterloo: Battle of Three Armies* (Book Club Associates, 1979), pp.200-1.
2. See Paul Dawson, *Waterloo, The Truth at Last* (Frontline, Barnsley, 2017).

The regiment that really turned the advancing tide of the Imperial Guard, the 52nd (Oxfordshire) Regiment of Foot (Light Infantry), in action during the final stages of the Battle of Waterloo. (Anne S.K. Brown Military Collection, Brown University Library)

A panoramic painting of the final stages of the Battle of Waterloo. Napoleon and his staff can be seen fleeing on horseback in the left foreground.

GONE BUT NOT FORGOTTEN ✦ NAPOLEON BONAPARTE

MAIN PICTURE:
Napoleon and his entourage on HMS Bellerophon, 15 July 1815.
(Anne S.K. Brown Military Collection, Brown University Library)

MIDDLE RIGHT:
Napoleon, followed by his small staff, is received upon HMS Bellerophon by the warship's officers.
(Anne S.K. Brown Military Collection, Brown University Library)

MIDDLE LEFT:
Described as the 'latest portrait of Napoleon', this portrait was completed by the artist Sir Charles Lock Eastlake whilst Bonaparte was onboard HMS Bellerophon.
(Anne S.K. Brown Military Collection, Brown University Library)

GONE BUT NOT FORGOTTEN

Napoleon's Enduring Legacy

It was not just Napoleon's soldiers who deserted him after Waterloo – the whole of France, it seemed, had abandoned him. When he escaped capture to reach Paris on 21 June 1815, he still hoped to rally support but, on the 22nd, the Senate and the Council of State told him that he had one hour in which to abdicate or be stripped of his title.

Napoleon, exhausted and shocked with the events of the previous few days, offered no fight, issuing a typically grandiose Napoleonic statement: 'Frenchmen! In commencing war for the maintenance of national independence, I relied on the union of all wills and all authorities. I had reason to hope for success, and I braved all the declarations of the powers against me. Circumstances appear to have changed. I offer myself as a sacrifice to the hatred of the enemies of France. May they prove sincere in their declaration, and have aimed only at me! My political life is ended.'[1]

With that he abdicated for a second time in favour of his son. Whilst the abdication was accepted by the two chambers, they refused to accept the King of Rome. Instead a provisional government was formed of five members until a permanent constitution could be established.

The insistence that Napoleon should quickly announce his abdication was prompted by the very real danger that he might be taken prisoner by the Prussian army which was pursuing the beaten French with relish. Blücher, for his part, certainly wanted

NAPOLEON BONAPARTE ⚜ GONE BUT NOT FORGOTTEN

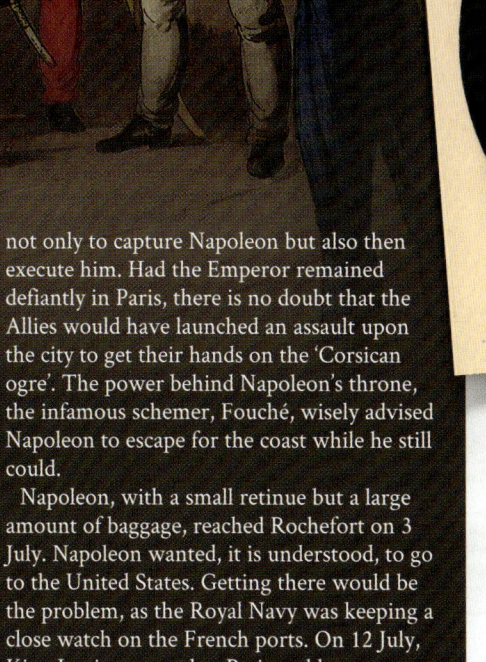

not only to capture Napoleon but also then execute him. Had the Emperor remained defiantly in Paris, there is no doubt that the Allies would have launched an assault upon the city to get their hands on the 'Corsican ogre'. The power behind Napoleon's throne, the infamous schemer, Fouché, wisely advised Napoleon to escape for the coast while he still could.

Napoleon, with a small retinue but a large amount of baggage, reached Rochefort on 3 July. Napoleon wanted, it is understood, to go to the United States. Getting there would be the problem, as the Royal Navy was keeping a close watch on the French ports. On 12 July, King Louis returned to Paris and he, too, wanted Napoleon's blood. The Emperor could not wait any longer.

He sent an appeal to the Prince-Regent for asylum in Britain through Captain Maitland of the Royal Navy's 74-gun warship HMS *Bellerophon* which was standing off Rochefort. Napoleon hoped, he is reported to have said, to live as a private individual in England. But there was no chance of this. He was to be removed to the securest, most distant and isolated spot that could be found from where there was no possibility of escape – the sparsely-populated volcanic rock that is the island of St Helena in the middle of the Atlantic Ocean.

Napoleon began his exile on St Helena in October 1815. He lived there in what was regarded as damp and unhealthy circumstances, in the house of the former lieutenant governor of the island, until, on 5 May 1821, he died of cancer of the stomach. Though he wished to be buried in Paris, this was denied by the Brutish authorities and he was interred on the island. His remains were eventually taken back to France in 1840, where they have remained to this day in a stone sarcophagus in the crypt under the dome at Les Invalides.

A Reforming Ruler

It may be recalled that this brief study into the life of Napoleon Bonaparte began with observing that his memory is kept very much alive in present-day Paris. Visually, this is certainly the case, with the Arc de Triumph still a major tourist attraction. Work on its construction began in 1806. Built to commemorate Napoleon's victories, it continued to be the focal point for triumphal marches of victorious armies – both those of France and its enemies – the last occasion being the victory march of the Allies in 1945. Almost as impressive is Napoleon's column in the Place Vendôme, built to commemorate his victory at Austerlitz. That battle is also still remembered in the railway station of the Gare d'Austerlitz.

Napoleon's legacy, however, goes far deeper than commemorative monuments. The French Revolution had swept away the old order, but had failed to replace it with lasting systems or institutions. This was in part due to the fact that France was almost continually at war during that period. Napoleon's victories brought a degree of stability that enabled him to create the foundations of many administrative and legislative bodies that continue in France to this day.

ABOVE: *Napoleon boards HMS* **Bellerophon.** *His rowboat can be seen drawn along the warship's starboard side with Napoleon himself climbing the steps to be met by Captain Frederick L. Maitland. Other ships are visible in the area, one of which may be HMS* **Superb.** *(US Library of Congress; LC-USZ62-26321)*

Gone But Not Forgotten   Napoleon Bonaparte

Perhaps the best known of these is the Civil Code, popularly known as the Napoleonic Code. The Code represented a comprehensive reformation and codification of the French civil laws. Under the *ancien régime* more than 400 codes of laws were in place in various parts of France, with common law predominating in the north and Roman law in the south. The revolutionary government overturned many of these laws, but then enacted more than 14,000 pieces of legislation of its own. So, to bring order to this chaos, Napoleon assembled a commission of legal experts to bring all these various pieces of legislation together in an understandable, uniform and accessible manner. At the heart of the Code were the fundamentals of equality before the law, freedom of religion and the abolition of feudalism.[2]

The Napoleonic Code was adopted throughout much of Continental Europe and remained in force after Napoleon's defeat. Napoleon himself once said: 'My true glory is not to have won forty battles ... Waterloo will erase the memory of so many victories ... But ... what will live forever, is my Civil Code.'[3]

It is certainly the case that more than twenty countries across Europe, the Americas and Africa adopted the Code as the basis of their legal systems. The Civil Code was actually only one of six codes, that codified commercial and criminal law – the Code of Civil Procedure in 1806, a Commercial Code in 1807, a Criminal Code and Code of Criminal Procedure in 1808 and a Penal Code in 1810.

The extent of his lasting reforms, considering the short time he was in power, is remarkable – such is the influence of a dictator, particularly a benign one such as Napoleon. He introduced a number of state secondary schools (lycées) to bring about a standardization of higher education; a tax code, road and sewer systems, and established the Banque de France, the first central bank in French history.

ABOVE: *A hand-coloured engraving depicting Napoleon's house on the island of St Helena from 10 December 1815 until his death on 5 May 1821. Longwood House lies on windswept plain some four miles from Jamestown.* (Anne S.K. Brown Military Collection, Brown University Library)

A drawing depicting a contemplative Napoleon Bonaparte during his exile on St Helena. (Morphart Creation/Shutterstock)

Longwood House, which was Napoleon's residence during his time on St Helena, as it is today. (Lisa Strachan/Shutterstock)

As we have seen earlier, he instituted the Légion d'Honneur, which is still France's highest order of merit, both civilian and military. The Légion d'Honneur is also awarded to deserving people from countries other than France. He was also responsible for the introduction of the metric system in September 1799, which has now been adopted by all but three countries in the world.[4]

The Military Leader

Despite the scope of his civil reforms, it is as a general that Napoleon is best remembered. His art of war and his memorable manoeuvres and battles are still studied, and hotly debated, at military academies.

Before the Revolutionary and Napoleon eras, the monarchies of Europe had waged war with armies they could neither adequately recruit nor pay for. There were two consequences of this. The first was that commanders took great care not to place

NAPOLEON BONAPARTE — GONE BUT NOT FORGOTTEN

their armies in situations where they would be compelled to fight in anything less than highly favourable circumstances, as they could not make up the numbers of men they might lose in battle. This meant that huge pitched battles were rare, and conflicts dragged on for many years. The second was that the war would eventually become too heavy a financial burden upon the warring parties, resulting in a peace that was rarely more than an unsatisfactory compromise.

Napoleon changed all of that. His aim was always to bring the enemy to battle in the shortest possible time with all the forces available to him. The bigger the battle, the greater the victory. His swift and devastating tactics shocked his opponents, but eventually they adapted, and committed huge numbers of troops to engage in battles on a vast scale.

Speed was possibly the most important ingredient in Napoleon's strategies, enabling him to out-manoeuvre his pedantic old-fashioned opponents. 'Strategy is the art of making use of time and space,' he once declared, 'space we can recover, time never'. 'I may lose a battle, but I shall never lose a minute'; 'The loss of time is irreparable in war'; 'Time is the great element between weight and force'.[5] Such were Napoleon's pronouncements on the necessity of speed.

There is a dividing line between the warfare of the old order and that of the eras that followed, with their emphasis on the destruction of the enemy as a fighting force regardless of the casualties than might be incurred – and that line was drawn by Napoleon Bonaparte.

Beyond France

Napoleon conquered many small states in Italy and Germany which were governed or powerfully influenced by larger countries with their peoples trapped in feudalism by their overlords. Napoleon swept the old order away in those countries and offered them the prospect of self-determination. When Napoleon drove the Austrians out of Italy, for example, he tried to unify the states he had taken. This was the first step in the long struggle for Italian Unification which became a reality in 1871.

Similarly, Germany was divided into a large number of states under the direction of the Holy Roman Emperor, which, since the fifteenth century, had always been the Hapsburg Archduke of Austria.[6] After the Austrian defeat at Austerlitz, Napoleon grouped sixteen (later thirty-five) of these states into the Confederation of the Rhine. With this, the title of Holy Roman Emperor became meaningless, and the Empire was dissolved by Francis II on 6 August 1806. After Napoleon's abdication, and the dismantling of the Confederation of the Rhine, Prussia was able to place itself at the fore of the German states, which came together, under Prussian leadership, to form the country of Germany that we know today.

Napoleon's intervention in Spain also saw the abolition of the Inquisition. He legalised divorce, closed the Jewish ghettos and made Jews equal to everyone else. 'The ideas that underpin our modern world–meritocracy, equality before the law, property rights, religious toleration, modern secular education, sound finances,' wrote one historian, 'were championed, consolidated, codified and geographically extended by Napoleon'.[7]

Napoleon also helped France's treasury with the sale of the Louisiana Territory to the United States. But the sale helped the US to an even greater extent, as this doubled the size of the existing US and paved the way for the further expansion westward in the decades that followed.

Napoleon's body, carried in a flag-covered coffin, passes through Lower Parade in Jamestown, the capital of St Helena, on 15 October 1840, as it begins its journey to France. (Anne S.K. Brown Military Collection, Brown University Library)

ABOVE: *In this watercolour by R. Brunton, two soldiers can be seen inspecting Napoleon's original tomb on St Helena. In his will Napoleon asked to be buried on the banks of the Seine, but the British Governor, Hudson Lowe, insisted he should be buried on St Helena, in the Valley of the Willows (now Sane Valley).* (Anne S.K. Brown Military Collection, Brown University Library)

ABOVE: *Napoleon's tomb on St Helena today.* (Lisa Strachan/Shutterstock)

GONE BUT NOT FORGOTTEN NAPOLEON BONAPARTE

A European Union

Napoleon has divided opinion throughout the last 200 years, being considered by some as a warmonger and by others as a great visionary. That latter view is, naturally, how Napoleon saw himself.

'I have cleansed the Revolution,' he told his secretary, Las Cases, on St Helena, 'ennobled the common people, and restored the authority of kings. I have stirred all men to competition, I have rewarded merit wherever I found it, I have pushed back the boundaries of greatness ... Is there any point on which I could be attacked and on which a historian could not take up my defence? ... My ambition? Ah, no doubt he will find that I had ambition, a great deal of it – but the grandest and noblest, perhaps that ever was; the ambition of establishing and consecrating at last the kingdom of reason, and the full exercise, the complete enjoyment, of all human capabilities!'[8]

Though clearly overstating his case, Napoleon brought order out of the chaos of the Revolution while maintaining its basic principles – and these he exported to other countries of Europe, showing the common people that they too could have liberty, equality and fraternity. He did indeed develop a meritocracy, somewhat flawed it must be confessed, but opportunities were there for people in a manner that had never been possible under the privileged Bourbon monarchy. This was exemplified in the French Army where it was said that 'every soldier carries a marshal's baton in his knapsack'.

At one time, Napoleon ruled or had influence over much of western Europe and, according to one of his statements, sought to bring the peoples of Europe together under one leadership. He explained his vision for the future of the Continent as follows: 'Europe thus divided into nationalities freely formed and free internally, peace between States would have become easier, the United States of Europe would become a possibility. I wished to found a European system, a European Code of Laws, a European judiciary; there would be but one people in Europe.'[9]

Does that all sound remarkably familiar? ❖

ABOVE: *Napoleon's tomb in Les Invalides, Paris. The return of Napoleon's body, an event known as 'la retour des cendres', was arranged by King Louis Philippe. His remains were first buried in the Chapelle Saint-Jérôme in Les Invalides, until his tomb, seen here, was completed in 1861. It was made using red quartzite and rests on a green granite base. (Shutterstock)*

ABOVE: *The coffin containing Napoleon's body arrives at the quayside in Jamestown Harbour, 18 October 1840, to be loaded aboard a ship for transfer back to France. (Anne S.K. Brown Military Collection, Brown University Library)*

RIGHT: *One of the most recognisable landmarks in Paris, the Arc de Triomphe de l'Étoile plays an important part in keeping the memory of Napoleon Bonaparte alive. On 15 December 1840, brought back to France from St Helena, Napoleon's remains passed under it on their way to his final resting place in Les Invalides. (Shutterstock)*

NOTES:
1. Quoted in Digby Smith, p.215.
2. See www.napoleon-series.org/research/government.
3. Bernard Schwartz, *The Code Napoleon and the Common-law World* (The Lawbook Exchange, Clark, 1998), p.7.
4. These three are Liberia, Myanmar and the USA.
5. All quoted in Chandler, p.149.
6. Apart from one brief spell between 1508 and 1519.
7. Andrew Roberts, *Napoleon: A Life* (Viking, New York, 2014) p. xxxiii.
8. Herold, p.390.
9. Quoted in Frank McLynn, *Napoleon, A Biography* (Pimlico, London, 1997), p.664.